PURE
Religion

A STUDY OF JAMES

Published by Gospel Advocate Co.
1006 Elm Hill Pike, Nashville, TN 37210
http://www.gospeladvocate.com

ISBN-10: 0-89225-559-5
ISBN-13: 978-0-89225-559-7

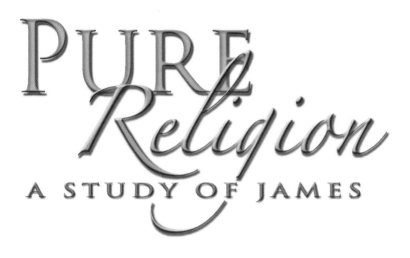

PURE
Religion
A STUDY OF JAMES

BY
DAVID BRAGG

Gospel Advocate Company
Nashville, Tennessee

DEDICATION

To my parents, Don & Mary Bragg,
and my in-laws, Jean Marilyn & the late Norman Hogan;
each is a special source of love and wisdom.

TABLE OF CONTENTS

FOREWORD

Upton Sinclair referred to a passage from James as the words of "a woman terrorist agitator," [1] or a rebel rouser whose inflammatory class-envy speech can result only in causing great harm for the poor they stir to action against the wealthy. As his voice bursts from this epistle, James calls for every Christian to consider seriously Jesus Christ and His will for them. He refuses to excuse shallow faith or turn a blind eye to professed believers giving less than their all to back up their public profession of faith. Christianity must be lived on a daily basis, even through life's trials and heartaches.

Sinclair identified precisely why this little letter has so often been seen as a threat to Christianity: James' challenge to his readers to "practice what they preach." Those who desire only a feel-good religion are in for a terrible shock as they read James' inspired treatise on "pure religion" and his refreshingly honest portrayal of faith, humbly obeying God's Word (James 1:21-22). The goal of his epistle is pure religion, described as an active response to God through Christ encompassing one's speech, acts of charity and rejection of sin (vv. 26-27). James enumerates barriers to this pure religion: trials, temptations, prejudice, inactive faith, uncontrolled tongue, earthly wisdom, worldly pleasures, arrogance toward God, and oppression. Any of these can be overwhelming and spell spiritual defeat. All of them can be overcome, as James eloquently demonstrates.

It is not difficult to see why James was such a beloved and respected leader among the early Christians. One of the greatest acts of wisdom by their successors was to include this little, yet powerful epistle where it rightfully belongs, alongside the other inspired writings of the New Testament.

David Bragg

CHAPTER 1

James,

THE MAN AND THE LETTER

voice of reason arose over the clamor that was threatening to drown out the young church of Christ. Some were insisting that the Jewish rite of circumcision be imposed on Gentile converts to Christianity as a condition of their salvation (Acts 15:1-2). Paul was adamantly opposing these measures, but it was James who led the parties to a peaceful resolution at the famous Jerusalem gathering (vv. 13ff). A brief letter was sent out to the Gentile converts informing them of the Jerusalem leaders' unanimous decision (vv. 23-29). Years later Clement of Alexandria described that letter as a "catholic epistle," [1] a title that would soon become the classification for the seven letters between Hebrews and Revelation. "These epistles are called catholic, universal, or circular, because they were not written to one nation or city, but to believers everywhere." [2] Unlike Paul's letters addressed to particular congregations or individuals, these letters were general in their scope, addressed to the universal church (so the terms "catholic" and "general" are appropriately applied).

The general epistles are named for their authors rather than recipients and are arranged in groups according to the listing of the "pillars" of the Jerusalem church (Galatians 2:9). James, the first of the general epistles, has been subject to mixed reviews. On the positive side it has been described as the "how-to book of the Christian life," [3] challenging the reader on to greater spiritual growth. Respected for its wisdom ("the Proverbs of the New Testament" [4]) and straightforwardness ("the Amos of the New Testament" [5]), it addresses life's everyday circumstances, showing the practical nature of true faith. It reaches to the believer's very core. "If the message of James is allowed to go out unmuffled, it will rattle the stained glass windows." [6]

In 2002, People for the Ethical Treatment of Animals took legal action against the California Milk Advisory Board for running their "happy cow" ads featuring "singing, wise-cracking dairy cows contentedly munching grass." The lawsuit claimed "the ads violate consumer protection laws by deceiving consumers about the way cows actually live." [7] Rest assured that James uses no trickery, no smoke and mirrors or hidden strings in his practical lessons. He describes how persons live when Jesus is Lord of their life.

On the negative side, James poses serious problems for interpreters, some arising from the letter itself and others from the scholar's own personal prejudices. Few men have done more to discredit James than Martin Luther, who called it, "a really dangerous book." [8] The letter was therefore subjected to a wide range of interpretations and more than its share of controversy. Some people approach the letter as one might approach the book of Proverbs, as a collection of independent, unrelated statements on the subject of divine wisdom. In their hands, James becomes "the rambling effusion of some indeterminate scribbler without plan, purpose, or authority." [9]

THE AUTHOR'S TRUE IDENTITY

Much of the controversy surrounding this letter involves the search for its author's true identity. James, the Greek form of Jacob (the patriarch whose name God changed to Israel), has always been a popular name. For example, three of the four women at Jesus' cross are known to have had sons named James (John 19:25; Matthew 27:55-56).

At most, six men in the New Testament are named James from whom the author of this letter will be found. Commentators vary on the exact number within this group. For example, James the son of Alphaeus (Matthew 10:3) and James the Less (Mark 15:40) are generally considered to be the same person (therefore making five men named James). Outside of being mentioned in the gospels and Acts 1:13, little is known about James the son of Alphaeus, and it is unthinkable that his name recognition was anywhere close to that of this letter's author. Likewise, nothing is known about James the father of Judas (Luke 6:16), who is not a serious candidate for authorship.[10]

The best-known New Testament James was the fisherman apostle, James the son of Zebedee. He was among the innermost circle of Jesus' apostles. However, James' early death at the hands of Herod almost certainly eliminates him as the author of this letter (Acts 12:1-2). Only a few individuals have advanced the theory that this James wrote the New Testament letter of the same name.[11] His support was strongest in Spain where James was their "patron saint." [12]

The two remaining men, James the Lord's brother (Matthew 13:55; Galatians 1:19) and James the brother of Jude (Jude 1), are almost unanimously identified as the same person and the author of this epistle. While this conclusion agrees with the evidence of the New Testament, it does not satisfy the creedal positions of some scholars. Therefore, intricate theories had to be adopted to navigate around these perceived obstacles.

One problem this James posed for the skeptics was his not being one of Jesus' apostles. Some of the earliest Christian scholars believed that authoritative books had to come from an apostle. A second problem came in trying to harmonize the word "brother" with the adopted doctrine of the perpetual virginity of Mary.

A few scholars (e.g. John Calvin) identify James the Lord's brother with James the son of Alphaeus, who was clearly an apostle, making him the author of James.[13] Various efforts to buttress their case include a theory making James the Lord's step-brother, Joseph's older son by a former wife,[14,15] or widening the definition of "brother" to include one's close relative. Supposing that James the Lord's brother, James the son of Alphaeus, and James the Less all refer to the same individual, an intricate theory was built around John 19:25 claiming that James and Jesus were actually cousins rather than brothers. However, when one compares Matthew 27:55-56 with John, it is clear that "His mother's sister" refers to Salome, the wife of Zebedee and the mother of James and John. That James was Jesus' cousin.

Jerome indicated another possibility – that an unknown person wrote the letter using James' name and reputation to promote it. The ethical problem of this theory did not occur to (or bother) "Luther, who ascribed the letter to 'some good, pious man who had taken some sayings from the apostle's disciples.' " [16] "Some good, pious man" who just happens to be a forger and dishonest? Even if one assumed that this was possible, what was his motive? James doesn't contain any of the common elements, miraculous accounts or strange doctrines of pseudonymous writings. "Why produce a non-polemical Jewish-Christian Epistle that is not even taking the position of the Judaizers but simply giving a call to 'practical religion' "? [17]

JAMES THE LORD'S BROTHER

The best option for authorship of this letter is James the Lord's brother (Matthew 13:55). Note the author's simple introduction of himself (James 1:1). When speaking "of a less commonly recognized individual with a common name, one usually added a qualifying title, e.g., 'Plato the comic poet.' " [18] Yet, James did not use any qualifying title to indicate that he was widely known. Instead, the reader is greeted with the simple statement of the author's submission to Jesus. "The highest claim that James makes (and its Greek position is emphatic) is that he is 'a servant.' " [19] Scholars have argued that if this James had been an apostle or the brother of Jesus, he would have said so in the opening verse. But the fact that he didn't appears to bolster the case for authenticity, especially when compared to how non-authentic documents introduce James. The Gospel of Thomas, a gnostic gospel from about A.D. 200, introduces James with the lofty "for whose sake heaven and earth came into being." In the Liturgy of Thomas, utilized in the Orthodox Church on the day set aside for the feast day honoring James, he is referred to as "the Brother of God." [20] And in the non-canonical "Epistle of Peter" (included in the Ante-Nicene Fathers), James is addressed as "the lord and bishop of the holy Church."

Henry Heitfeld was "a rather unambitious candidate" who never voted for himself. One day, having voted for someone else, Heitfeld sat quietly at his desk keeping track of the votes being cast. Recognizing that he was receiving an unusually large number of votes, Heitfeld stood at the conclusion of the roll call with this request: "Mr. President, I desire to change my vote. I vote for Heitfeld." The chamber suddenly erupted in laughter, thinking it was a joke. When the official results were announced, Heitfeld had been appointed to the U.S. Senate, beating his nearest rival by a single vote.[21] The world's all-too-human attitude is reflected in, "I vote for myself." James could have promoted himself easily and truthfully. Instead he chose to present himself in a humble manner, not flaunting his credentials but recognizing the close bond he enjoys first with the Lord then with his readers, who are admonished to be faithful servants of Christ.

To get to know James, one should meet his father, whom Matthew describes as a "just man" (Matthew 1:19). Obviously Joseph and Mary reared all of their children in "strict observance of the Law of Moses." [22] Joseph's noble traits were especially evident in his treatment of Mary before and after their wedding. James was likely the first son born to the couple after Jesus' birth (he is always listed first among Jesus' siblings, Matthew 13:55). One can assume that the various advantages provided to Jesus as He matured under the guidance of Joseph and Mary would have been available to James. After being reared in a godly Galilean home, James married and established a Galilean Christian home (1 Corinthians 9:5). He was not one of Jesus' disciples (Luke 8:19-21; John 7:5). While Jesus was dying on the cross, the care of Mary was committed to John rather than to His unbelieving eldest brother (19:26).

A sudden change occurred after Jesus' resurrection when His brothers are numbered with the disciples (Acts 1:13-14). Paul traces the sudden change to Jesus' post-resurrection appearance to James (1 Corinthians 15:1-7). As the missionary momentum shifted away from the Jerusalem church and Luke's focus turned to the work of Paul in the Gentile world, James emerged as a strong leader, a "pillar" (Galatians 2:9) in the Jerusalem church. His close association with Paul permitted their participation in benevolent projects to relieve the poor in Jerusalem (2:10; Acts 21:18-19). On Paul's last recorded visit to Jerusalem, James suggested that he participate in a ceremonial vow to demonstrate his allegiance to the Jewish Law (vv. 20-26). In keeping with his philosophy, Paul agreed. For James, this occasion revealed his close connection with Jewish Christians. It gave Paul's enemies the opportunity to arrest him, leading to his eventual voyage to Rome.

Although James became an established leader of Jewish Christians, he never encouraged the kind of prejudice that fueled the circumcision controversy of Acts 15. "James was not 'a Jewish Christian'; he was a Christian Jew. 'Christian' is the adjective, 'Jew' the noun – the thing that he was – and leadership of Jews in particular, not of Christians in general was his clear goal." [23] As a leader among the Christian Jews, James was a missionary to the Jews, but he was not associated with the Judaizers. "The Ebionites were an extreme early Jewish-Christian sect who rejected the Pauline Epistles and regarded James as their patron, falsely supposing that he was in opposition to Paul. Eusebius says that their name, meaning 'the poor ones,' exhibits the poverty of their intellect." [24] That James encouraged any such activity is never indicated.

The Jewish historian Josephus describes the murder of James, which occurred in A.D. 62. After the death of the Roman governor Festus and before the arrival of Albinus his successor, the Jewish high priest Ananus unleashed his anger against the church in a three-month reign of terror. The Jews "reenacted the tragic scene of death under the charge of blasphemy formerly used against Jesus and Stephen, but this time with James the Brother of Jesus as the victim." [25] After being thrown from the pinnacle of the temple by the Pharisees, James was stoned and beaten to death with a launderer's club. Once Governor Albinus arrived, he was greeted by renewed outrage over the Jewish persecution of the church.

> The high priest who had done the deed was deposed by the new Governor, but the Governor … organized his own pillage, set prisoners free for fees, and allowed the Sadducees free rein in Jerusalem; mobs ran riot … . He was exceeded in the audacity of his misrule only by his successor Florus (A.D. 64-66). Meanwhile the Romans were growing tired of the bickering and the attacks upon the Roman supply trains. Vespasian was on his way to set the troubled province at peace. The rest is tragedy.[26]

The tragedy would come in the form of Rome's destruction of Jerusalem. "There would seem to have been quite a widespread conviction among both the Christians and the Jews that the afflictions which fell upon the holy city and the chosen people in the following years were in part a visitation because of the great crime of the murder of this just man." [27]

QUESTIONS, RUMORS AND A LEGACY

Many of the questions left unanswered in the New Testament became fodder for the fanciful storytellers of extra-biblical documents. Among these writings are spectacular claims, such as the story of James "being cured of a snake-bite by the infant Jesus" (in the "Gospel of the Infancy, by Thomas the Israelite philosopher" [28]). Eusebius, the church historian, preserved Hegesippus's description of James, who was called "the Just" (A.D. 180). He claims that James was a Nazarite from his mother's womb and that he did not use the bath. James was a man of constant prayer, and although he was not a priest under the Jewish Law, he was permitted to enter into the holy place. He was "found there frequently upon his knees begging forgiveness for the people, and his knees became hard like those of a camel in consequence of his constantly bending them in his worship of God and asking forgiveness for the people." [29]

If there were an award for the most unusual business venture, it would have to go to Akira Hareruya, who in 1999 walked out of his bankrupt electrical contracting company and onto the streets of Tokyo with a pair of boxing gloves. For the equivalent of $9 a minute, the 36-year-old allowed pedestrians to punch at him (promising not to hit back, only to evade their punches) and, to further relieve stress, they could yell at him as they punched. He reportedly was making about $200 a night.[30] In a similar environment of hostility, the epistle of James came to the forefront of the Jerusalem church, and critics have been taking swings at it ever since.

But to the church, and especially in Scripture, James was a man of incredible influence, not because he was the Lord's brother but because he was, as his daily life demonstrated, the Lord's servant. "The Jews respected him, and the Christians revered him. No man among them commanded the esteem of the entire population as much as he." [31] James was known as the defender and protector of the poor and consequently was hated by the ruling rich, who were often the subject of his rebuke (James 5:1ff). "Jewish Christianity looked back to James as its hero and leader." [32] His greatest legacy rests in the words that flowed from his life, directed by the Holy Spirit, presenting the timeless lessons that will forever occupy a cherished place in the New Testament between Hebrews and 1 Peter.

STUDY QUESTIONS

1. What is a catholic epistle?

2. Construct a list of all the men named James in the New Testament and give a brief description of each.

3. Which of these men can be ruled out as the author of this epistle? Why?

4. What preconceived views influenced scholars in identifying the author of this epistle?

5. How does John 19:25 enter the issue of authorship?

6. What is the significance of John 7:5 in the debate of James' authorship?

7. Which best describes James: a Jewish Christian? a Christian Jew? a Judaizer? Why?

8. Explain James' role in Acts 15.

9. How does Josephus depict James?

10. How is James depicted by Hegesippus?

CHAPTER 2

AN *Unusual* JOY

(JAMES 1:1-11)

"The two most abundant things in the universe are hydrogen and stupidity." [1] Although there are obvious limits to human intelligence, there are no such limits on stupidity (Proverbs 26:4-11). "[Modern society is] awash in a sea of ignorance," wrote Michael Turner in the *Chicago Tribune*. "We know much and understand little." [2] This makes it even more important for the Christian, who holds the map to the strait and narrow path of life (Matthew 7:13-14), to put his knowledge into practice as James constantly urges.

James' reference to "the twelve tribes" (James 1:1) appears to identify his audience as Christian Jews. This seems to be supported by the words "scattered abroad," which translate a technical word, "diaspora." That word has historically been used to describe the involuntary deportation of Israelites. Others point out that nothing in the letter indicates that James' appeal is restricted to a Jewish audience. Although he makes several appeals to the law, in the context of each he points the reader to the teaching of Jesus rather than that of Moses (v. 25; 2:8, 12).

Luther objected to the letter's "unevangelistic nature." If James had addressed a purely Jewish audience, the letter might be portrayed as fostering prejudice. Instead, James addressed only Christians, without regard to their ethnic roots and without making an appeal to the unconverted world.[3] The "twelve tribes which are scattered abroad" probably refers to Christians who are dispersed throughout the world making their journey toward their homeland (pilgrims, Philippians 3:20; 1 Peter 2:11). Cloaked in this Old Testament imagery, James writes to the new "spiritual Israel of God, that is, the Christians of all ages" [4] (Galatians 3:28-29; 6:16; Romans 2:28-29; 4:11-12).

If James the Lord's brother is the author of this letter, then it was written before A.D. 62, the year of his murder. James played a key role in the Jerusalem meeting in A.D. 49. Because neither the Jerusalem meeting nor the controversy concerning circumcision is mentioned, it is thought that James was written before that time (A.D. 44-49), making it the first document of the New Testament. One interesting theory is that this epistle is the Jewish counterpart to the Gentile letter of Acts 15:23ff. [5] Others prefer to follow the "sounder judgment" of William Sanday, who places the letter as late as possible in James' life.[6] While absolute certainty is impossible, James was probably written between A.D. 45-62.

Like Hebrews, the style of James resembles a sermon. It begins with the elements of an epistle – the author's name, audience and a formal greeting – but then its form tends to follow that of the popular Greek diatribe. James presents his thoughts in question and answer style with imaginary opponents, a style that would have great appeal to his original readers.[7] Whether letter or sermon, the practical lessons of James hold obvious value for those seeking spiritual nourishment.

Although James did not believe Jesus was the messiah during His earthly ministry, the fact that he remained close to his older brother is evident. At least 26 allusions to the Sermon on the Mount are made in James, more than the rest of the epistles combined.[8] Many critics question James' authenticity and even the early church's awareness of its existence, but "the language and thought of James are so interwoven into the fabric of the earliest Christian writers (just as James does with the thoughts of Jesus) that it seems clearly to have been a part of the reading and hearing of the church from the beginning." [9] The lessons James teaches arise from his very person, not as an apostle or even the Lord's brother, only a humble bondservant of Jesus Christ (James 1:1). "The skeptic became a servant. And he wasn't ashamed to say so!" [10] The implications of James' autobiographical description are impressive: absolute obedience, absolute humility, absolute loyalty, and a certain pride of belonging to Christ.[11]

JOYOUS GREETINGS

One indication of authenticity is the unusual word, "Greetings," which literally means, "Joy be to you." [12] A common greeting outside the New Testament, it is rarely found inside: once in a letter to Felix (Acts 23:26) and again in a letter from James (15:23). In the Greek text, the word "greetings" is immediately followed by the words "all joy" ("full and complete joy" [13]). James emphasizes his theme of joy by using this joyful salutation. From the standpoint of the unbelieving world, James demonstrates that the maturing Christian possesses the most unusual joy. Unlike the superficial joy of the world, this joy is not conditioned on circumstances, emotions or external forces. It is grounded in the Christian's very soul, so that when his life is littered with unhappy trials, he can still retain his joy.

It quickly becomes clear that James selected his words carefully and intentionally (James 1:1-12). "My brethren," a favorite, tender address to his audience (used 15 times), introduces a call for them to make a judgment about those circumstances in life beyond their control. They are to count these trials with joy. Their response must be based on what they know rather than what they see (2 Corinthians 5:7). The word "trials" can describe hardship or persecution, "a trial of any kind." [14] In this case James clearly has external trials in mind, the kind that one "falls into," of which there are many ("various, of many kinds" [15]).

James presents three key thoughts relating to one's joyous outlook toward trials.

• **Christians must expect to face hardship.** At the beginning of 2003, the National Safety Council reported that each year the average American faces a "1 in 2,844,716 chance of death from a 'fall into a hole or other opening in the earth's surface.' " [16] Few people make plans to avoid this unlikely occurrence. But the chances that a Christian will face hardship are 100 percent, so he can prepare. Jesus (Matthew 5:11-12), Paul (2 Timothy 3:12; 1 Thessalonians 3:4) and Peter (1 Peter 1:6-7; 4:12-13) consistently taught the reality of suffering. For James it isn't a matter of if one will be tried, but when.

• **Life's unexpected hardships should be greeted with joy.** James and others modeled this teaching before the church and the world (Acts 5:41; 16:23-25; 2 Corinthians 7:4; Colossians 1:24). "The thing which amazed the heathen in the centuries of persecution was that the martyrs did not die grimly, they died singing." Barclay relates one particular case in which the martyr was seen smiling as he was burned to death. When asked why he smiled his reply was, "I saw the glory of God, and was glad." [17] Christians can retain full joy even in adversity because of Jesus' promise never to leave them (Hebrews 13:5-6).

• **The first victory over any adversity must take place in the mind.** James pictures the Christian sorting through his various life experiences. Each time adversity is encountered, the Christian intentionally places it in the "joy" category. To reinforce his point, James begins verse 3 with the word "know," which indicates a "knowledge obtained through ... personal experience." [18] With complete trust in God's promises, the Christian can view hardship with joy (2 Corinthians 4:16-18; 5:7). Adversity is an opportunity to grow.

THE ROLE OF ADVERSITY

Reuben Gonzolas won his first professional racquetball tournament with a spectacular shot the defending champion was unable to return. The judge immediately declared Gonzolas the winner, and the line judge confirmed the call. But after Gonzolas conferred with the officials, their ruling was reversed, and his opponent declared the official winner. Soon Gonzolas' picture was on the cover of the leading racquetball magazine, and its opening editorial struggled to explain why he did it. Gonzolas' explanation: "It was the only thing I could do to maintain my integrity." [19]

James tells his readers that the way they handle life's trials will either confirm and strengthen or deny and dismantle their integrity as Christians (1 Peter 1:6-7; Job 23:10; Psalm 66:10). This is true whether one's struggle is internal (with temptation, James 1:12; thoughts about others, 2:1; what to say to others, 3:9-11, 4:11; what is said to God, v. 3) or external (actions, 1:27; 2:15-16; 4:10; boasts, 4:13). James describes the purifying process of meeting and mastering the various trials of life as a "testing" (1:3). He used the Greek word *dokimos* ("the genuine element" of one's faith[20]) that was also used to describe the difference between pure gold that had been processed for coinage and impure gold from which the dross or impurities had not yet been removed.

James states that the diversity of trials one faces in life will provide a multitude of opportunities to prove or test the genuineness of their faith (James 1:2). As Christians stand up under these heavy burdens, they will experience spiritual growth, exhibiting qualities similar to those found in their Redeemer upon whom they rely for strength and guidance. James may have borrowed the words "perfect" and "complete" in James 1:4 from his knowledge of Jewish "sacrifices under the law,"[21] where an acceptable sacrificial animal was healthy and whole. "Lacking nothing" could be used of a person or object that has achieved or served its intended purpose, goal or standard.[22]

Certainly the most important word of James 1:2-4 is the word "let" (v. 4). The reader has the ultimate choice whether the trial will prove or break him. If Christians are not strengthened by trials, it is because they do not "let" endurance produce its perfect result. Adversity makes maturing Christians stronger because they know the promises they cherish will outlast any adversity they will encounter in life.

THE ROLE OF WISDOM

Once again James ties his thoughts together with carefully selected words. Using a form of the word rendered "lacking nothing" (James 1:4), James tells his readers that if any of them lacks wisdom (v. 5) they should turn to God with their needs. He recognizes the difficulty in striving for this goal (cf. Philippians 3:12-16). By repeating the word "lacking," James is asking the reader to consider, "How can this trial be used for good?"[23] The wisdom of which James speaks consists of more than just facts; as one writer stated, "one may be a 'walking Bible' and not be wise."[24] This wisdom is very personal. Wisdom has been described as "the practical use of knowledge,"[25] "true religion" (cf. James 1:26-27[26]); and the quality of knowing and practicing righteousness.[27]

Because all truth is revealed in the complete Word of God (John 17:17), certainly James is not promising some form of direct, personal revelation from God. While adversity can draw the Christian closer to God by making him aware of the deep need for Him, one must always rely upon God's Word to know how best to deal with life situations and remain pleasing to Him. It remains the prerogative of the believer to make the first move by realizing his need for wisdom and making the request of God. "He who does not ask thus does not feel his need of Divine teaching. The ancient Greek maxim ... is literally true ... 'The knowledge of ignorance is the beginning of knowledge.' " [28]

A request for wisdom must be made in the confidence of three promises. The first is that giving comes naturally to God, and He will give wisdom liberally. Although "men often complicate and mar their giving," [29] when God gives He shows not even the hint of reluctance. Second, God gives "without reproach." He does not humiliate or scold when giving "lest anyone should fear to come too often to God." [30] The third promise is that sincere petitions will be granted (Matthew 7:11; 1 John 3:22; 5:14-15).

THE ROLE OF FAITH

From the human perspective, the prayer for wisdom must be "in faith, with no doubting" (James 1:6). Faith is essential to Christianity (Hebrews 11:6; 2 Corinthians 5:7). As James uses it here, faith is the unwavering trust in God exhibited by the suffering Christian who derives strength from Him while awaiting the ultimate promises available only in Christ. This unwavering faith is contrasted with a familiar scene from nature, the boat on a storm-tossed sea (James 1:6).

In 2003, Adrian Cross set out to break the world record for sailing around the world (just over 64 days). After 130 days he had not even made it out of the English Channel. The newspaper story began, "A British yachtsman has abandoned his round-the-world voyage after taking twice the time needed to circumnavigate the globe just to leave the English Channel." Cross recalled, "We've been like a cork in a washing machine." [31] The one who wavers in faith is even worse than a cork. Not only is he going nowhere fast, his prayers aren't even taken seriously. God says in reply to these pleas, he "shall not receive anything," much less wisdom (James 1:6b-8).

James depicts the "double-minded" man (James 1:8, literally "two souls," a word James probably coined [32]) as one who is trying to "serve two masters" (cf. Matthew 6:24). His soul is divided between heaven and earth. James' sea metaphor in verse 6 helps illustrate this hopeless plight. "At one time cast on the shore of faith and hope, at another rolled back into the abyss of unbelief; at one time raised to the height of worldly pride, at another tossed in the sands of despair and affliction." [33] Such a person is undependable in every area of life, and such a Christian, James says, has been found unworthy of God's trust.

THE ROLE OF WEALTH

In a contrast between the eternal and temporal, James compares two Christians, one who through no apparent fault of his own is poverty stricken, and the other one who is rich (James 1:9-11). The poor Christian is generally despised by the world, but in Christ he is elevated to a position of great honor as a priest (1 Peter 2:4-5), a king (Revelation 1:6) and a fellow heir with Christ (Romans 8:17). The rich are honored by the world; even the church is tempted to show them inappropriate favoritism (James 2:1-4). But the challenge for the maturing Christian who happens to be wealthy is humility (1:10-11) and reliance upon God rather than wealth (Jeremiah 9:23-24). Both Jesus and Paul recognized the danger of placing one's trust in material wealth which, like the grass and flowers of the field, will not last (Matthew 6:19-20; 1 Timothy 6:10). No matter what status the world may assign to individuals, in Christ they are brothers and sisters.

From these trials, true joy emerges in James 1:12. "Blessed," a word for "religious joy," [34] are the victorious Christians who have endured their trials, trusted the promises, received the wisdom, and now stand approved ("something tried and proved genuine" [35]). Their ultimate joy will be receiving the promised crown from Him. The crown is "the victor's wreath," [36] a common figure in apostolic letters (1 Corinthians 9:25; 2 Timothy 4:8; 1 Peter 5:4), symbolizing the eternal life and joy awaiting the faithful Christian. God blesses even through the varied trials of life and ultimately with eternal joy.

STUDY QUESTIONS

1. To whom was this letter addressed?

2. In what should Christians find joy?

3. What does James mean by various trials?

4. What will testing produce?

5. Why can man ask and receive wisdom from God?

6. How must one ask for wisdom? Why?

7. Who will not receive wisdom? Why?

8. In what situations should the poor and rich rejoice?

9. How does James depict material wealth?

10. How is a man blessed by trials?

CHAPTER 3

Heart TROUBLE
(JAMES 1:12-18)

The original readers of James wouldn't have understood the dangers of high cholesterol, clogged arteries or aneurisms. They did not have the medical knowledge to converse intelligently on a technical level with the modern medical world. But their lack of knowledge didn't keep them from dying from heart disease.

While the readers of James couldn't grasp discussions about the physical heart beating in their chests, they could understand the kind of heart trouble that James described in James 1:12-18. James again demonstrated his affinity for just the right word as he makes the transition between the "trials" of verse 2 and the "temptation" of verses 12 and 13 (using a form of the same Greek word in both passages, a noun in verse 2, *peirasmon*, and a verb in verses 12-15, *peirazomenos*, the two words being derived from *peiraz*[1]). The most popular interpretation of these words is that "trials" refers to an outward circumstance[2] while "temptation" refers to the "inner impulse to evil."[3] Clearly James has two closely related but distinct concepts in mind as Chapter 1 unfolds.

OUTWARD TRIALS

God, in allowing humanity the opportunity to make incredibly good and wonderful choices, of necessity makes incredibly bad and inhumane choices possible. On a practical level, the trials of life represent the challenge of deciding one's values, the moral course of life, and ultimately his eternal destiny. God has not isolated His people from the ravages of life. When met in a positive manner, those external trials have a beneficial place in the Christian's life, resulting in the maturing of his or her faith (James 1:3-4). Matured faith will then be manifest in the following areas: drawing closer to God for wisdom (v. 5); growth in commitment (vv. 6-8); and preparation at any moment for eternity (v. 12).

Friends and family of Margaret Long McCullough, an active member of the church in Tupelo, Miss., honored her at an open house in celebration of her 90th birthday. On that occasion her son, Glenn, reminisced about growing up in the McCullough home saying that his mother, who seldom missed a congregational event, took him out of worship services so regularly to spank him that he grew up thinking there were "six items of worship" rather than the five most of us think of.[4] While strong examples of parental discipline are greatly appreciated, the need for it is especially evident in its absence (Proverbs 29:15, 17; 13:24). Solomon's observation in Proverbs 3:11-12 is of special interest to the Hebrews writer, who quotes it in Hebrews 12:5-6.

Is James or the writer of Hebrews saying that God, as our Father, intentionally designs hardships to send into the life of individual Christians for the specific purpose of maturing their faith? Such an interpretation seems similar to the Iranian proverb, "If you see a blind man, kick him, why should you be kinder than God?"[5] Not only does it tend to paint a less-than-accurate portrayal of God and His love, but it also poses a problem for Peter's assertion that God is no respecter of persons (Acts 10:34). The inspired writers are not delving into the cause (or origin) of the trials they discuss (Hebrews 11:5-11); they are simply content in seeing the hand of God when their faith is tested and rejoice at the opportunity to prove their love for Him.

Unlike the personal interaction of the Patriarchal Age when Abraham was clearly tested by God (Genesis 22:1), the focus of the Christian Dispensation rests on God's complete and inspired Word (Hebrews 1:1-2). Christians rely on the New Testament (8:7-13) rather than on direct revelations from God. A case can be made, however, for God's use of hardships in life to prove the true worth of one's profession of faith (12:5-6). Although God is not necessarily pictured as the source of these trials, He clearly encourages mankind to use them for good (1 Corinthians 10:13; Romans 8:28). It appears then to be slightly more accurate to conclude that the song of thanksgiving to God that arises from the furnace of suffering is not for the trials He brings upon the Christian but rather for the trials He brings them through. It is the outcome rather than the origin that James has in view.

INWARD TEMPTATION

When properly approached, as outlined by James in the previous verses, adversities can be looked upon as a blessing. If they hadn't faced those hardships, Christians might not have grown in patience and faith or possessed the compassion that enables them to serve others more effectively. James 1:12 can be used as a key transition verse because, without inflicting harm upon the text, the word "temptation" can and should be interpreted both ways (as outward trials and inward struggles). Just as Christians strive to overcome the outward trials, trusting God's promise of eternal life, so also must they do battle with their inward trials, the temptation to sin, knowing that the same promise is attached to that victory as well. Whether tempted or tried, James shows that Christians always have a clear path to God. When tempted to sin, they must first gain the victory over their personal will, desire and mind.

Sadly, sometimes one responds to trials by rebelling against God. Rather than bringing out the good, a trial that posed an opportunity to grow can also bring out an evil response. James 1:12 might just as easily address the topic of the inward struggle with sin. The motivations are the same whether one struggles with an external hardship or an internal brawl over good and evil. Those who are victorious will be stronger, more mature Christians and will, being approved at life's dusk, receive the crown of life. This is the wonderful motivation to make the mental choice, when faced with temptation, to follow the path etched out by James. Be warned – what he advocates is not easy. As William Beckford said, "I am not over-fond of resisting temptation." [6] Temptation is real (1 Corinthians 10:13), common to all (1 Peter 5:8-9), and can be overcome (2 Peter 2:9).

Regarding temptation, James uses the word "when," not "if" in 1:13a. There is a certainty when it comes to the universal struggle against sin.

All Christians will be tempted. While God may be associated with the external trials of life (vv. 2-12), it is an insult to attribute one's temptation to sin as coming from God. From Eden a clear pattern is established of blaming others, even God (Genesis 3:12-13), and failing to take responsibility for one's sin. Not only is such a person deceived, but he has also deceived himself.

James sets out to demonstrate that it is impossible for a holy God to be responsible in any way for man's inward struggle with sin. "He never tempts a man to commit any form of evil. He Himself has no dealings with evil, and He does not entice to sin." [7] Although the word "tempted" is similar to the "trials" of verse 2, the context clearly establishes that James is considering one's inward "solicitation to evil." [8] James denies that God has any role in the temptation process. "[Henry] Alford translates the final clause, 'nor does He Himself tempt anyone,' according to the ordinary sense of the Greek, 'God is unversed in evil.' " [9] If not God, then what is the source of temptation?

THE SOURCE OF TEMPTATION

An unusual "help wanted" ad was placed in the Staffordshire, England, newspaper. The historic Shugborough Home was seeking to fill the position of hermit; they needed someone to live temporarily in a cave on the property and frighten away any trespassers that may happen to enter the property. [10] But even if one were to live away from all contact with the outside world, he or she would still not escape the source of temptation (James 1:14). The response of blaming others, claiming that sin is a sickness, or any other ruse designed to avoid personal responsibility for sin is taken away by the inspired writer who identifies the sole source of temptation as the individual. Satan's role is not mentioned so that readers can focus on their own personal responsibility. James "tracks the lion to its den when he says: 'Each one is tempted when he is drawn away by his own desires and enticed.' Sin comes from within us." [11]

James attributes temptation to following one's desires or lusts. These are natural impulses unnaturally expressed.[12] The appetite for food is not sinful, for example, in its natural context. Only when these desires are abused in a manner displeasing to God do they play the role described here as temptation. This is the oldest form of heart disease (Matthew 15:19-20a). After the source is identified, James turns his attention to the process of temptation.

The practical approach adopted by James is to trace the process of temptation backwards, illustrating how it should be addressed as a thought before it manifests itself in sinful behavior. "Even Satan's suggestions do not endanger us before they are made our own." [13] Sin does not automatically happen. There is a thought process in which choices are weighed, values sifted, consequences measured, and paths determined. Clarke illustrates this with a Jewish proverb: "Evil [desire] is, at the beginning, like the thread of a spider's web; afterwards it is like a cart rope." [14] At this early stage, the sinful thought quickly rejected would save untold sorrow. "Instead of expelling the vile thought, we may encourage, nourish, and enjoy it." [15]

James asserts that Christians are not helpless when tempted to sin. The sinful thought can be ejected, surrounded by the "it is written" fortress in the same way Christ dealt with temptation (Matthew 4). One can purposely fill his or her mind with the proper thoughts of Philippians 4:8 and meditate upon the truth rather than nurture the temptation. During the early stage, while temptation is but a mere thought, the Christian has the best opportunity for victory. The first battlefield of temptation is in the mind. But the process is blurred by man's deception concerning the temptation process itself, which James describes in very colorful terms.

TEMPTATION'S HERITAGE

Temptation's heritage is derived from her grandmother, personified by James as "Desire" (1:15). She is portrayed "as the harlot that allures the man," [16] drawing him away from God's truth. Who would have imagined that any harm could come from a tiny desire? Although small and seemingly harmless, Desire can almost immediately spawn the most hideous offspring, Sin, who is born ready to bring forth its child, Death (James 1:15; Romans 6:23). With great skill, James draws a striking contrast between the Christian who is victorious over external trials (James 1:2), growing in patience (v. 3) and receiving the crown of life (v. 12) with the Christian overcome by the evil desire within himself that consequently produces the malignancy of sin and ultimately death (v. 15).

Temptation involves being "drawn away" (James 1:14), a hunting term describing the hunter coaxing prey out from its cover and into the snares.[17] The first step is for the child of God to be "drawn away from truth and virtue." [18] Once one's mind has been distracted from God and His will, he can be easily "enticed," a fishing term meaning, taken with a bait, like "a fish swimming in a straight course and then drawn off towards something that seems attractive, only to discover that the bait has a deadly hook in it." [19]

Because sin always "leads to eternal, spiritual death – the final separation of the person from God," [20] the battle against it is primarily spiritual. When it comes to waging war with the devil, every human is severely outmatched (Ephesians 6:10-18). Man's only hope is in Jesus. Relying on that hope, James warns against self-deception (James 1:16). One must properly recognize the source, responsibility or even the result of sin (each sinner is "the ancestor of his own demise" [21]). The seriousness of this warning may rest in the original language that calls upon James' readers to stop their current practice of being deceived over who is really responsible for their sins.

James again asserts that, because of His holy nature, God cannot be involved in temptation (James 1:13, 17). God provides only "good (useful, practical) and perfect (nothing lacking in them)" gifts.[22] The word "gift" appears twice in verse 17, but two different Greek words are used. The first, "good gifts," depicts the act of giving while the second word means, "the thing given." [23] James is clear that God gives only good because only He is good. That has to be the final word on His role in the source of man's temptation to sin.

As James contemplates the goodness and holiness of God, he provides his readers with a list of God's inherent qualities. God is the Creator of all things, including the vast universe with the sun, moon and other heavenly bodies ("the Father of lights," James 1:17). Just as the sun is the source of light, God is the eternal source of good. He is changeless. There is "no variation or shadow of turning" with Him. This phrase might refer to the shifting shadows caused as the sun moves throughout the day or the "declining brilliance" of the sun.[24] Either way, what the sun experiences, God doesn't. He is the instigator of salvation ("Of His own will He brought us forth," v. 18). Although humans struggle between embracing evil desires or the will of God, the Creator voluntarily chose to establish a plan for their redemption, including the most perfect Gift of His Son (John 3:16).

GOD'S RESCUE

The contrast between God's will to save mankind and sin's will to destroy them is illustrated in James' careful choice of words. The verb, "brought us forth" (James 1:18), has the same root as the word translated "brings forth" in verse 15. Sin births death while God gives humanity the chance to be born again. God made true life possible through Jesus (1 Peter 1:23). James draws a stark contrast between the new birth of death in James 1:15 and the life-giving new birth of baptism (James 1:18; Romans 6:1-4).

When David Urey's wife was dying as a result of a tragic automobile accident, doctors on the scene offered little hope for her survival. Urey was told she required immediate neurosurgery if she were to live, but there was no way to get her to those services in that area of West Virginia. He tried to charter a helicopter to lift her to Washington, D.C., but to no avail. In desperation he called the White House. Perhaps President Nixon could help. Somehow Urey got through. Before long Nixon's private helicopter arrived to assist.[25]

James speaks of a far greater rescue. In man's greatest need, God by His own will came to the rescue through Jesus Christ. Because He did, Christians now have become "a kind of firstfruits of His creatures" (James 1:18b). While in the Old Testament the "term 'firstfruits' referred to the first portion of the harvest given to God (Deut. 18:4; Num. 18:12; Ex. 13:11-16" [26]), James uses the phrase figuratively of "people ... because they were a guarantee of many more to come." [27] James concludes his first 18 verses on a note of strong optimism. He knows for certain that God's Word will prevail and that those who know the love of God will embrace Him and share the good news with others so that they too might gain the final victory over sin and death.

STUDY QUESTIONS

1. What is the distinction between trials and temptations?

2. How does temptation come about?

3. Explain the significance of the phrase "drawn away."

4. What is the significance of the word "enticed"?

5. Why does James not mention Satan in connection with temptation?

6. What is the end result of temptation?

7. What kinds of gifts come from God?

8. How is God's changeless nature described?

9. How are Christians "born again"?

10. What does James mean by his use of "firstfruits"?

CHAPTER 4

Christian EVIDENCE

(JAMES 1:19-27)

Although it may appear that James 1:19 begins a new line of thought, it is actually a powerful application of his previous lesson on outward trials and inward temptations. When trials are overcome, they lead to life (v. 12). When temptations overcome, they lead to death (v. 15). The same Word through which Christians found their new birth will be the basis for their new life. Within this context, James probes the intimate question of how the readers should receive God's Word (vv. 19-21), apply its principles to their personal lives (vv. 22-25), and live it before an unbelieving world (vv. 26-27). What role should the Word of God play in one's life? At baptism every newborn Christian accepts, along with salvation from sin, the responsibility for spiritual growth that requires learning and living God's Word (2 Timothy 2:15).

The first few words in James 1:19 lend themselves to two appropriate translations, as is evident by comparing the "So then" of the New King James Version, which simply conveys the reader to a new thought, to the New International Version's command, "[T]ake note of this." The NIV powerfully charges the readers "to be sure to practice their faith by the specific behaviors listed in this section." [1] Spiritual maturity can be obtained only by following the three crisp commands that reflect the individual responsibility of every Christian – "let every man be swift to hear, slow to speak, slow to wrath" (James 1:19 NKJV).

INDIVIDUAL RESPONSIBILITIES

• **Swift to Hear.** The charge to be "swift to hear" recognizes the impossibility of learning without listening. When God speaks, the wise will, as James instructs, "Hurry up and hear!" [2] Socrates, the great Greek philosopher, once charged a pupil a double fee. When asked why, he explained, "I shall have to teach you two sciences; first, how to hold your tongue, and second, how to use it." [3] Individuals must be eagerly receptive to what God has said through His written Word. With the modern proliferation of the Bible, it is hard to appreciate the fact that in James' day most "did not possess their own personal copy of the Scriptures. Most of them were dependent upon hearing it read (see Nehemiah 8:1-8; 1 Timothy 4:13)." [4] Failure to comply with the command to be swift to hear results in a Christian living closer to the world than to God's Word and, being content with past study, growing weak and stagnant in his faith.

After having ignored seven warnings, the ill-fated *Titanic* finally recognized the danger it faced. Only a few hours before, the *Titanic*'s radio operator upbraided his colleague on the nearby *Californian* for interrupting him with another warning. As a result, when the man on the *Californian*'s shift ended at 11:30, he turned his radio off, thereby missing the urgent plea for help that came soon after midnight. The *Titanic* sank while only 10 miles away the *Californian* drifted silently along, no longer listening.[5] Listening is a vital skill in every area of human interaction, and listening to God's Word and to one another is a vital part of Christianity.

• **Slow to Speak.** By James' admonition to be "slow to speak" (literally, "slow to begin speaking," James 1:19), the Christian is cautioned against proclaiming the Word before first practicing it [6] or perhaps the greater danger of speaking back to God, "show[ing] displeasure at the teachings of the word." [7] One may "talk back" to God by resisting, twisting or simply neglecting what He demands of him as a Christian.

Taken together, these first two commands in James form the basis for success in every area of life. Not only are these concepts emphasized within Scripture (Proverbs 10:19; 13:3; 17:28; 29:20), they are also stressed in secular writings. "Nature has given to man one tongue, but two ears, that we may hear from others twice as much as we speak." [8]

"The ears are open and exposed, whereas the tongue is walled in behind the teeth." [9] "I have sometimes had occasion to regret that I have spoken, never that I was silent." [10]

• **Slow to Wrath.** A Christian possesses a teachable spirit by listening to God, reflecting upon His Truth, and then responding with an attitude of true faith. This is what James means by his command, "slow to wrath." The Greek word for "wrath" describes a "violent emotion resulting in uncontrolled anger," [11] more precisely, "a state of mind not an emotional outburst." [12] Once again, by his careful selection of words, James has illustrated an important point by drawing his reader's attention to the thoughts behind their actions. "A person who is careful to consider what he says, is not likely to be soon angry." [13]

While some understand this admonition as a reaction to one's fellow man, the context indicates that James has in mind one's reaction to God and His Word. The response must be free from anger, not lashing out at God because of one's trials. Such anger betrays a faith that has failed the test (cf. James 1:3), and it hinders one's obedience to God. This person cannot work righteousness, which is the state a sinner enters at the point of initial forgiveness when one becomes "acceptable to God." [14] As James next observes in verse 20, being "slow to wrath" is impossible for the man who has surrendered to his own anger. Anger in the Christian's life burdens and distracts, diminishing one's ability to teach the lost.

THE BATTLE AGAINST SIN

Even after conversion, the Christian continues to wage a battle against sin. To that end James outlines the journey toward spiritual maturity. This will require the removal of sin from one's life, replacing it with God's Word. The Christian must "lay aside" some things, the typical word for the removal of clothing or "of a snake's shedding his skin and leaving it behind." [15] Christians are to "lay aside all filthiness" (James 1:21). The Greek word translated "filthiness," *ruparian*, is derived from *rupos*. When used in a medical context, this word "means wax in the ear … James is telling his readers to get rid of everything which would stop their ears to the true word of God." [16] The Christian is to remove every form (mental or physical) of filthiness as one would remove soiled garments (James 1:21). The motivation is a sincere desire to please God (1 Peter 1:14-15). In his phrase "overflow of wickedness," James calls for the removal of desires and actions designed to hurt others. He describes these desires as an "overflow," or excess, a "tangled undergrowth or a cancerous growth, which must be cut away." [17] James calls for nothing less than a complete departure from sin.

Having taken a clear stand against sin, the Christian must use God's Word to fill the void that removal creates. This requires a teachable heart willing to receive the Word with meekness, "without resistance, disputing, or questioning." [18] Meekness stands in contrast to wrath and describes one's control of emotions and conformity to God's Word. James calls that Word "implanted," which some define as "innate as opposed to acquired" [19] (like the Gentile's conscience; Romans 2:14-15) while others say it is planted like a seed. The second meaning is preferred because one receives God's Word only through instruction (Romans 10:14). That which is born within a person does not need to be received (i.e. one's conscience). God's Word, however, is often portrayed as being sown in the hearts of men (Matthew 13:1-9, 18-23).

DOERS OF THE WORD

Properly received by one possessing a clear desire to be cleansed from sins, the sown Word possesses the power to save the soul. James is not advocating a passive acceptance of God's Word. Like Paul in Romans 2:13, James calls for a careful hearing followed by sincere application of the inspired principles of Scripture in the life of each individual (James 1:22). Rather than letting God's Word "go in one ear and out the other," hearing but not changing, Christians must "be doers" of the Word. James' word "hearers" was used for those "regular in listening to lectures, but who never became real disciples." [20] The solution is not to stop listening but to start consistently obeying God's Word.

According to a December 2002 Canadian federal court ruling, the Bible is "hate literature." [21] At issue were four passages denoting homosexuality as sin. If the Bible is merely words and not God's Word, such a conclusion might make sense. But Christians know better. God's Word must be obeyed. Faith in Christ will place this obedience as first priority in the Christian's heart.

To illustrate, James draws a parallel between the Bible and a mirror, which in his time consisted of "polished metal," silver, copper, tin, or "Corinthian bronze" [22] (James 1:23-24; cf. Exodus 38:8). The man he portrayed looks at his reflection ("a fleeting glance" at "the face of his birth" [23]). As he stands gazing at his reflection, he is clearly dissatisfied with what he sees, wants to be different, and may even form steps to make serious corrections. However, once he turns away from the mirror, he is immediately distracted to other things and forgets all about what he saw in the mirror and his plans to reform.

Just as that man "derives no benefit from the mirror," [24] the inactive Christian, who should be looking in the Word to correct his life, profits nothing from hearing it. Quickly it is heard and just as quickly discarded without having changed or benefited that hearer. God has given His inspired will so that, when application is made, one will live a better, happier life that is pleasing in His sight. Christians must practice the truth in their daily lives and relationships (Matthew 7:21-23; Luke 6:46; 11:28; John 12:48; 15:14). Again, James' choice of words impresses the reader with the importance of God's Word. The students are to "look intently" into God's Truth,[25] put the principles learned into practice in their lives, and share them with others.

The Christian faith is described as "the perfect law of liberty." There is no contradiction in this phrase because liberty is not the complete absence of rules; only anarchy can exist without laws and rules. The New Testament is a law consisting of rules and commands (Galatians 6:1-2; Hebrews 7:12; 8:10); it is perfect because it is God's final revelation (1:1-2), complete and mature in every way (2 Timothy 3:15-17). No additional revelation is required, only loving obedience (John 14:15). "Sin must have a law to transgress, because that is what sin is (1 John 3:4), and love must have a law to obey because that is what love does (1 John 5:3)." [26]

While many follow Luther's lead in questioning James' introduction of works as they relate to daily Christian living, James has no hesitancy in asserting that true faith is always active and productive. The forgetful hearer is contrasted with those who practice in their daily life what is learned from God. Their service is an expression of love to God and results in both immediate and ultimate blessings.

A WORTHLESS RELIGION

It started out as a great idea. Thailand's Department of Rights and Liberties Protection hired a street theater group to perform various skits "to encourage people injured while performing good deeds to ask for assistance from the government." During their performance on a crowded Bangkok street one Saturday afternoon, a police sergeant patrolling the area heard a woman's cry for help. Someone had stolen her purse. Seeing the purse-snatcher fleeing the scene, the policeman followed in hot pursuit, tackling the suspect, never realizing that he was just an actor. "I didn't know it was a play," he later told reporters. "I just heard a woman calling for help. I tried to hold him but he resisted. So I had to hurt him." [27]

At times the line between real and pretend may be difficult to discern. James 1:26 encourages Christians to take a close look into their hearts and lives. Do they hold only the illusion of faithfulness, being among the deceived of verse 22? Such persons only seem to be religious. One who "thinks he is religious" bases his conclusion only upon "his own estimation." [28] Because his life is inconsistent with his claim of faith, such a person plays a trick of the very worst kind because "any behavior inconsistent with the Christian faith is worthless." [29] His religion is vain "because it fails to please God, which should be the primary object of religion." [30] God appraises it as a shell with no substance.

When James speaks of religion in the closing verses of Chapter 1, he uses a word that describes the outward expressions of worship. He is talking about "what the observer sees taking place in church." [31] Having exposed vain religion, James now outlines true religion and the evidence of true Christianity's presence. Behind the actions of public worship, James describes the faith of the doer as "pure and undefiled," words describing the positive and negative side of purity.[32] Three examples are stated: speech, service and departure from sin.

The profession of faith by the hearer-only is betrayed by the failure to control speech. The failure to "bridle his tongue" leads again to self-deception, rendering religion useless. "A man can scarcely seem to be religious" when the faith he professes on Sunday is refuted by his words and actions on Monday.[33]

James' second example relates to the compassionate care extended to those in need, orphans and widows specifically. These were among the most defenseless because "neither [had] direct means of support nor automatic legal defenders in that society." [34] The Christian's obligation is to visit them; "it takes the oversight of them, it takes them under its care" so as to "alleviate their distresses." [35] James calls for the opposite approach adopted by the Pharisees (Matthew 23:14). Christians are to serve others after the pattern of Jesus. God, the ultimate judge of one's religion, says that the "externals of religion … are quite unacceptable to Him unless accompanied by a genuine desire on the part of the worshipper to render sympathetic and practical service to his fellow-men." [36]

Finally, the Christian must always strive to remain free from sin (James 1:27). The word "and" ("and to keep oneself unspotted") is not in the Greek. "[S]o close is the connection between active works of mercy to others, and the maintenance of personal unworldliness of spirit, word and deed." [37] By striving to remain "unspotted from the world" (which recalls the dirty clothes of James 1:21), the worshiper is free to draw near to God. The world James has in mind is the realm of Satan, the world of evil that is in rebellion against God (1 John 2:15; James 4:4). The responsibility of each individual is to keep oneself unspotted because pure "religion is of such a nature that no man can learn it but by experience." [38] Obedience not only blesses the individual, but it also pleases God. He is the only One who can ultimately approve one's religion.

James is obviously not limiting one's religion to concern for the fatherless and the widows. As Micah said in the Old Testament (Micah 6:7-8), these actions become the symbolic representations of a general approach to godly living suitable for every generation. As He examines the life of the faithful Christian, God should easily be able to identify the evidence of pure and undefiled faith.

STUDY QUESTIONS

1. In what must Christians be swift and slow? Why?

2. What is the Christian to lay aside?

3. What is meant by "overflow of wickedness"?

4. What does James mean by "meekness"?

5. What is the significance of the implanted word?

6. How can one deceive himself or herself?

7. What man is blessed by his actions? Why?

8. What is a trait of vain religion?

9. What are the traits of pure religion?

10. Who is the ultimate judge of religion's purity?

THE AWE OF

RELIGION

(JAMES 2:1-13)

When James wrote his epistle, he did not use the chapter and verse divisions found in modern Bibles. These valuable aids first appeared in Robert Estienne's Greek New Testament in 1551 [1] and in the Elizabethan Bible of 1557 in English.[2] Because it was added later, the chapter division does not accurately reflect James' thought division.

Pure religion couples its public demonstration with matching conduct (James 1:26-27). Vain religion has only the public demonstration.

> A brilliant summer morning, still & hot;
> A day for flannels & a pipe, & not
> For stuffy Sunday clothes, a long, dull walk,
> And duller sermon, & the vapid talk
> Of fellow-Christians, with souls replete,
> Hurrying to fill their bodies with roast meat.
> Their worship's over; God's returned to Heaven,
> And stays there till next Sunday at eleven.[3]

The public life of this worshiper contradicts his profession of faith. Although many hear the Word, they do not make a personal application of it to their lives (James 1:22). "These verses comprise the bedrock on which the whole epistle rests." [4]

James illustrates the contrast of vain and pure religion with a common example of human prejudice. The very heart of pure religion rejects the idea of prejudice. Building upon his example of pure religion as expressing compassion toward widows and orphans, James offers an example of showing respect of persons. The harsh topic is softened, and equality is stressed by the address, "My brethren," a subtle reminder what (and Whom) the Christian represents. Some in the world judge "the faith," the Christian religion, by the lives of those professing to believe.[5]

Although in the Greek the words "the Lord" are not in the phrase, "the Lord of glory" (James 2:1), James is referring to Jesus and intending to recognize Him as completely divine (Hebrews 1:1-3; John 17:5). He who was Himself poor by the world's standards (Matthew 8:20) is now exalted to the highest position of glory (Philippians 2:9-11). No human being or material object must ever be permitted to eclipse His glory in the eyes of the church and the individual Christian.

Therefore, each Christian holds "the faith of our Lord Jesus Christ" before a skeptical and unbelieving world. James is completely convinced that Christianity is more than words and worship; it is a life that confirms by deeds everything preached from the pages of Scripture. A closer examination reveals that James' words are honed as a specific rebuke to forbid a current practice. James is saying, "Stop showing favoritism." [6] This is not a hypothetical situation James has stumbled onto by chance. He is commanding them to stop a current practice.

What does it mean to show partiality? As James will show, it is the practice of judging people based solely on their look, dress or social status. The judgment is inappropriate because it is based solely upon their transitory nature (James 1:9-11). The Greek word James uses for "partiality" (*prosopolemphiais*) appears to have been created within Christianity because it is not found prior to its Christian use. [7] It means to "lift up one's face," to show another favor because of appearance. If prejudice is tolerated, an inevitable climate of "snobbery and caste distinctions [that is] utterly inconsistent with true Christianity" is certain to follow. [8] The long-term impact of partiality is even more dangerous. It distracts the church from the truly surpassing glory of Christ and discourages the world from obeying because they hear a message of love and brotherhood but see shameless pandering to the rich and powerful.

TWO VISITORS

In James 2:2, the Christian assembly is described using "the Greek [word for] synagogue." [9] This may suggest that James wrote to a Jewish audience, but it should be remembered that this was a common word for a gathering and that the basic use of the word had no religious connotation; it could refer to either the building or the people gathered. Although it was used for the church only once in the New Testament, many examples of such usage by other early Christian writers are found in their works.

The scene James paints has two unknown men entering the local church meeting. Immediately opinions are formed about them based solely upon their outward appearance and their dress. Most notable about the outward appearance of the wealthy man are his gold rings. In the culture of James' day, a man's ring served as his seal used to validate contracts as a kind of personal signature and as a sign of social status. The richer a person was, the more rings he wore. It was not uncommon for a man to rent rings if he wanted to leave the impression that he was rich. Rings were worn on the left hand (on the right hand was considered effeminate [10]), on all fingers except the middle, and multiple rings on each finger.[11] According to James, such a man enters the Christian assembly with expensive gold rings and wearing "fine apparel" or brightly colored clothes that grab the attention and perhaps even the envy of "those less endowed." [12] The second visitor wears garments that are dirty, reflecting his poor station in life.

Having introduced the two characters, James next sketches the troubling reactions of the church to the presence of these two visitors. Gathering to worship in the name of "the Lord of glory" (James 2:1), the church is distracted by the sudden presence of the rich man in all his glory. They stumble all over themselves to show him honor and pay attention to him, indicating that the focus of the meeting has shifted away from Jesus, the Lord of glory. Everything screeches to a halt as the guest is escorted to a good seat. It is possible that the word "good" in verse 3 refers to their conducting the guest toward the seat ("Sit here, please" [13]). In contrast to the gregarious welcome afforded the wealthy man, the poor man is met only with curt, rude orders about where he is permitted to occupy space. As the church members swarm about their unknown wealthy visitor, making sure he is comfortable, their only concern towards the anonymous poor visitor is that he not get in their way or interfere with their more important guest.

THE INCOMPATIBILITY OF PREJUDICE AND PURE RELIGION

Prejudice results in creating partial judges with "evil thoughts" (James 2:4). The phrase "shown partiality" can mean "doubt" (as in 1:6). These Christians were causing doubts to arise in their own minds by their inconsistent actions. James reminds his readers, who are prejudging others, to be sure to remember their identity as Christians.

The other possible meaning, and the most likely, is that in prejudging they were creating class distinctions within the church. In passing judgment based solely on outward appearance, they have "become judges with evil thoughts" (James 2:4), reasoning wickedly as they categorize the value of another based on outward appearance, unlike God who judges the heart (1 Samuel 16:7). They have become judges when they should have remained worshipers, distracted from His greater glory by the rich man's inferior glory, swept away by a misplaced awe. As James places this serious situation before his readers, one can expect him to provide a solution for their misplaced reverence. Before doing so, he presents three reasons why their behavior is completely incompatible with "pure religion" and must not be tolerated.

• **Prejudice is contrary to God's judgment because it dishonors the poor man whom God has honored** (James 2:5-6a). James, like others (Matthew 11:5; Mark 12:37; 1 Corinthians 1:26-29), argues that the poor tend to obey the gospel more readily than the wealthy. Greek scholars agree that James probably wrote, "[T]hose poor in respect to the world," subtly indicating that although they appear to be poor, are "rich in faith and heirs of the kingdom."

Prejudicial Christians are found in the most awkward of positions, despising those whom God has honored. In passing this judgment, they find themselves and God on opposing sides. A third-century martyr named Lawrence refused to join a corrupt official's plot to extort money from the church. Given three days to collect a bribe, Lawrence gathered instead a group of the poorest members and, when his persecutor demanded to see the treasures, "valiant Lawrence, stretching out his arms over the poor, said: 'These are the precious treasure of the Church; these are the treasure indeed, in whom the faith of Christ reigneth, in whom Jesus Christ hath His mansion-place.' " [14] God values all men, including the poor that some Christians despise.

• **Prejudice is not acceptable because it is contrary to common sense** (James 2:6b-7). James is not making a blanket statement about the worthiness of the rich, but as a class, the wealthy have shown reluctance to obey the gospel and proved to be hostile toward those who have become Christians.

James traces three specific trials back to the rich. First, the rich oppress Christians (James 2:6b). Because many members were among the poor, they would be, as a class, subject to such harsh and unfair treatment. James' use of the word "oppress" indicates the position of power the wealthy held over the poor. Second, they "drag you into the courts," which implies their use of physical force against the poor (Acts 9:1-2; 16:19). Third, the rich heap blasphemy against the church. The early Christians seemed happier to endure the physical attacks against them than the verbal assaults made against their Lord. The phrase, "that noble name by which you are called" (James 2:7), refers literally to the "beautiful" name that is "called upon you." [15]

• **Prejudice is contrary to the "royal law"** (James 2:8-11). As he clearly asserted in Chapter 1, Christians are bound to a higher law than the Jew. What James previously referred to as "the perfect law of liberty" (1:25) he now calls "the royal law," which is to love one's neighbor (Leviticus 19:18; Matthew 22:36-40).

James warns his readers against using the royal law to sanctify their prejudices (James 2:8-9). Some might claim that their actions toward the rich visitor were simply expressions of love as the royal law demanded. Will they be consistent in that law by showing the same love toward the poor visitor? James will not permit his readers to mislabel sin as personal judgment. Prejudice is sin because it is contrary to the whole spirit of Christ and whoever practices it "works sin." [16] They have violated God's laws.

In addition to consistency, keeping the law demands perfection. Many of the Jews believed that they were considered righteous if the number of observed laws equaled or exceeded the number of laws broken. Rabbis historically argued against this viewpoint, saying, "[A]ny one sin has the seeds of all others in it," [17] or the Law is like a chain, "break one link and the chain is broken" [18] (Galatians 3:10). James illustrates his point by contrasting two of the Ten Commandments, one observed and the other transgressed (James 2:11). The result is the same as if every commandment had been broken; the violators are transgressors. Therefore, to show favoritism, even unintentionally, is to stumble.

THE ROLE OF MERCY

A certain man deviously joined the orchestra of the emperor of China. For years he posed as a flute player even though he couldn't play a note. Then the emperor requested a solo performance from each of his musicians. The imposter tried everything to evade the king's request. Seeing no other way out, on the day he was to perform he committed suicide, giving rise to the saying, "He refused to face the music." [19] Try as one may, there is no way to escape the approaching judgment before God. Those temporarily distracted from the surpassing glory of Christ by the fleeting glory of the rich must be reminded of the wonderful promises that await them as God's children. It is imperative for each Christian to "speak and … do as those who will be judged by the law of liberty" (James 2:12). The judgment James envisions is not just in the distant future. The verb rendered "will be" (*mello*) in verse 12 denotes imminent retribution. [20] "Christians ought to conduct themselves as if judgment may come at any moment." [21]

James offers a brilliant depiction of the crucial role mercy plays on behalf of the faithful Christian. With no merit from any human effort, those belonging to Christ are promised mercy while the rest of humanity face divine justice (James 2:12-13; cf. 2 Corinthians 5:10). The statement "judgment is without mercy" has been characterized as "vindictive and sub-Christian. But this is not so. Judgment, as judgment, is merciless. The moment it shows mercy it ceases to be pure judgment." [22] James personifies these two divine traits, and while "judgment threatens condemnation, mercy interposes and prevails over judgment. … When we are in danger of being condemned, she rises up and pleads for us, and covers us with her defence [sic], and enfolds us with her wings." [23] At judgment mercy triumphs; she cries out loudly on behalf of the believer. Jesus is not only the glory; He is also the mercy that will enable the believer to rejoice when judged (Romans 8:31-39; Matthew 9:13).

A survey, conducted on behalf of Universal Pictures, revealed the top 10 fears of Britons. In an age where terrorism is constantly in the news, their number one fear was spiders. Terrorism came in second, snakes third, heights fourth and rounding out the top five: death.[24] The list's ranking seems out of order. So also do the priorities of James' original audience. He has brought his readers, ancient and modern, to stand in awe of Jesus' glory. In light of his hypothetical illustration of how prejudice distracts Christ's church from His mission, James argues that now is the time to make every effort to be sure that one's faith is sincere and active. Christians must make sure their lives are consistent with their professions of faith and that their religion is pure. Only then can one confidently embrace the wonderful promises that await the children of God.

STUDY QUESTIONS

1. How should the Christian faith not be held?

2. What does a prejudiced person become?

3. Whom has God chosen and for what?

4. What is the result of prejudice in James' example?

5. How have the rich generally treated the church?

6. What is the royal law?

7. How can one be guilty of the whole law?

8. What example does James use of this principle?

9. How should Christians speak and act?

10. How is God's judgment meted out?

CHAPTER 6

James

AND THE FAITH-ONLY CONTROVERSY

"We ask by God's grace and love that we be forever remembered as those that bound together the hearts of two families to form a family of freedom in America." So reads the solemn truce officially bringing to an end the legendary feud between the Hatfields of West Virginia and the McCoys of Kentucky.[1] Fighting erupted between the two families on Aug. 7, 1882. By 1900 "more than 100 men, women and children had been killed or wounded."[2] The exact cause of the hostility is probably forever lost to history although "theories range from post-Civil War animosity to a stolen pig to a romance unacceptable to the families."[3] The last two surviving combatants from the famous feud met in 1976 for a "hatchet-burying" ceremony. The more recent truce was drafted by non-combatant family members, who have also hosted four Hatfield-McCoy Festivals. These highly commercialized ventures capitalize on the suffering their ancestors endured and inflicted. Despite the published truce, those names will always be linked with violence.

As one reads the practical wisdom packed into James' five short chapters, it is hard to believe that this little volume would pose a threat to anyone with a sincere interest in progressing toward spiritual maturity. Yet Martin Luther, a leading figure of the Protestant Reformation, described this letter as "worthy of no regard … fit only to be burnt"[4] and "a really dangerous and bad book."[5] In the pages ahead, some of the controversies mentioned in the previous chapters will be examined more closely.

THEORIES ABOUT THE AUTHOR

One major problem for critics revolved around the letter's author. The search to find which James wrote the book of James delved into the meanings of very common words like "apostle," "brother" and "cousin." Ultimately the search narrows to James, the Lord's brother, who was not one of the 12 apostles. James has been portrayed as "an intriguing, somewhat shadowy character." [6] Various theories have therefore been advanced to explain the heritage of this New Testament writer.

• **The Hieronymian View.** The Hieronymian view holds that James was a cousin of Jesus. This theory, first advanced by Jerome in A.D. 383 (his Greek name was Hieronymos), "proceeds from the erroneous assumption that the word 'apostle,' used to describe James in Galatians 1:19, can only refer to one of the twelve Apostles of Jesus." [7] Jerome thought the James of Galatians 1:19 and 2:9, and the author of the epistle were all to be identified with James the Less. His claim that James was not a literal brother but only a relative (a cousin) was based on carefully dissecting John 19:25 (discussed in Chapter 1).

This theory was unnecessary for two important reasons. First, Jerome ignored the fact that the New Testament writers had a Greek word for "cousin" at their disposal and didn't need to incorporate distant relatives into the term "brothers" (Colossians 4:10). Second, one can be recognized as an apostle without being one of the twelve (Barnabas, Acts 14:14).

The "Western Church accepted uncritically Jerome's counter-view that the 'brothers' were cousins of Jesus" [8] and that James was one of the 12 apostles of the gospels. In taking this position, they further entrenched their doctrine of the perpetual virginity of Mary, therefore distorting Scripture to advance a human doctrine.

• **The Helvidius View.** The literal interpretation, called the Helvidius view (named after Jerome's literary opponent [9]), asserts that James was the firstborn son of Joseph and Mary after the miraculous conception and birth of Jesus. Those opposed to this view objected that Jesus' brothers, including James, did not support Jesus during His earthly ministry, openly resisted Him, and even questioned His sanity (Mark 3:21; John 7:5). Although Jesus' brothers clearly rejected His Messianic claims, they remained close to Him and seemed "deeply impressed by His moral earnestness and by the fresh and fuller emphasis that He gave to certain aspects of the moral law enshrined in Scripture." [10] After His resurrection, all barriers between Christ and His brothers were completely dismantled (Acts 1:13-14).

The Jewish historian Josephus identified "the brother of Jesus, who was called Christ, James was his name." [11] Like Paul in Galatians 1:19, the phrase "the Lord's brother" served as a kind of nickname for James. [12] "Though it is not necessary to the thesis of authorship ... or the genuineness of the book of James, it may safely be concluded that James is an actual brother of Jesus in the flesh through the common mother, Mary." [13] Unfortunately, opposing views that sought to protect their cherished but unauthorized views regarding Mary's perpetual virginity successfully silenced those holding the literal interpretation, resulting in the diminishing influence of James' epistle.

• **The Epiphanian View.** The Epiphanian view was named after "Epiphanius in the fourth century," [14] who offered this "tortuous [series of] arguments" after Jerome's successful suppression of Helvidius. The Epiphanian view claims that James was the older son of Joseph from a previous marriage. One account asserts that James was 94 years old at the time of his death, making him nearly 30 years older than Jesus. [15] Others think Joseph had children as the result of a levirite marriage. The "necessary supporting evidence" for this theory came in the apocryphal book of James (Proevangelium). This "pre-Gospel" account tells a fanciful story of the miraculous birth and life of Mary, including her marriage to an elderly widower named Joseph. "There is no evidence for the theory except legend. Its real motivation was to supply a basis for the doctrine of the perpetual virginity of Mary." [16]

LUTHER'S OPPOSITION TO JAMES

Just as those who fought so diligently to protect the human doctrines regarding Jesus' mother, Luther's opposition was grounded solely in his determination to protect his doctrine of justification by faith only. This, he was persuaded, was clearly taught by Paul in Romans and Galatians (letters he heartily endorsed) and, he was equally persuaded, was denied by James.

One of the earliest references to James is Origen's commentary (A.D. 231) on John 8:24: "If faith is spoken of, but is without works, such faith is dead as we read in the current Epistle of James." [17] James is clear that true faith must be active. In this he agreed perfectly with Paul and all other inspired writers. Yet, Luther failed to appreciate that fact. From his famous "tower experience," [18] Luther thought he could finally resolve the longstanding conflict between his own imperfection (Matthew 5:48) and lack of sufficient "good works to satisfy God's demand for righteousness" [19] as he suddenly discovered salvation by "grace only" in Romans. James' emphasis on a "working faith" contradicted that conclusion, he thought.

Luther promoted only those New Testament books that seemed to support his conclusions (especially Romans, Galatians and Ephesians), saying, "[T]hese are the books which show thee Christ, and teach thee everything that is needful and blessed for thee to know even though thou never see or hear any other book or doctrine." The books that did not appear to support his teaching were opposed, especially James, of which Luther wrote, "Therefore is Saint James's Epistle a right strawy Epistle in comparison to it." [20] He derived the image of "straw" from 1 Corinthians 3:12-13, hinting that it would not withstand the test of time or eternal judgment.

It is important to keep Luther's methodology in mind. The following is his own explanation for rejecting James: "Accordingly, if [Holy Scripture] will not admit to my interpretations, then I will make rubble also of it. I almost feel like throwing Jimmy into the stove … ." [21] Luther did concede that James had some value as it contained "many a good saying," and upon that ground included it at the back of his Bible. Having abandoned the goal of seeking the Truth, Luther's study was confined to supporting and defending his own beliefs.

LUTHER AND "FAITH-ONLY"

After his "tower experience," Luther was convinced that one was justified before God through a passive submission, faith only. He saw James' assertion that "a man is justified by works" (James 2:24) as contradicting Paul, who wrote that "a man is justified by faith apart from the deeds of the law" (Romans 3:28). To reconcile the "apparent" contradiction, Luther simply rejected the epistles that appeared to disagree with the position he had adopted.

To add further support to his doctrine, Luther literally added the word "only" to Romans 3:28. Despite inspired warnings of the greater responsibility of a teacher and against mishandling God's Word (James 3:1; Revelation 22:18-19), "Luther underlines 'without the works of the law' by adding the adverb 'alone' … For this 'addition' to the text he was severely criticized by some." [22] Luther's change was "an unwarranted and unjustified rendering without lexical support." [23] He, however, dismissed his critics as "making a tremendous fuss because the word *sola*, 'alone', is not in Paul's text," [24] seeing his addition as a necessary clarification of Paul's intended meaning.

A Catholic priest, Luther was growing increasingly dissatisfied with the abuses going on around him. Pope Leo X and the Archbishop of Mainz were both engaged in the buying and selling of "spiritual" offices or benefits. During this period, indulgences were sold that promised to grant complete forgiveness of sins for either the purchaser or for a friend, whether living or dead. "A popular jingle of the time phrased the promise well: As soon as the coin in the coffer rings, The soul from purgatory springs." [25] Proceeds from these sales went to the Archbishop of Mainz and the construction of Saint Peter's Cathedral in Rome. For Luther, to discover that salvation is the free gift from God, not something to be purchased from the church or its leaders, was a joyful revelation. But in reacting to the perverted system of earning works toward one's salvation, Luther erred.[26] Unfortunately, he dramatically over responded in setting forth his doctrine of justification by faith only.

Luther's problem was a failure to understand the nature of the works that Paul rejected in Romans and Galatians in regard to justification. The apostle was opposing those who sought to earn salvation by keeping the Mosaic Law (Romans 3:28-31). No man can be justified by keeping the Jewish Law, only by obeying Christ in faith. Paul perfectly agrees with James, who is addressing the problem of Christians who mistakenly think they have earned salvation through mere mental assent to the gospel and therefore have no need to do anything else. So James equates "faith only" with an inactive faith (James 2:24-26).

AGREEMENT BETWEEN PAUL AND JAMES

If only Luther had studied James more carefully, he would have realized that Paul and James are in complete agreement. There is not a single contradiction in their respective letters. "Paul's affirmation that we are justified 'by faith' and James' declaration that we are justified 'by works' mean simply that we are indeed justified 'by both,' and that it is a sin to assert that men are justified either (a) 'by faith alone,' or (b) 'by works alone.' " [27]

However, the doctrine of "faith only" that Luther helped to instigate continues to comfort and mislead countless souls who may have otherwise obeyed the simple gospel of Christ. It is unlikely that Luther would agree with the modern denominational doctrine of "faith only," that contends "justification is by faith without works of any kind" [28] (Romans 4:1-6). In 1520, Luther published a work titled "On Good Works" in which he argued, "[G]ood works necessarily flow out of a life of faith but are a result of and not the basis for man's justification, which depends entirely upon God's grace." [29] He also wrote, "[I]t is just as impossible to separate faith and works as it is to separate heat and light from fire." [30] When James calls upon his readers to be "doers of the word, and not hearers only" (James 1:22), he is agreeing perfectly with Paul (Romans 2:13). Although he misunderstood James, Luther agreed with the letter he so despised, eloquently writing: "We are justified by faith alone, but not by the faith which is alone." [31]

Modern proponents of "faith only" reject the biblical teaching on baptism, labeling it as "works salvation." "But Luther himself emphasized the importance of baptism." [32] Unfortunately, the passing of time has only added to the confusion and polarization in denominational camps in an effort to protect a human doctrine as if it were divinely ordained. Luther's mistake is perpetuated generation after generation. Consider the following texts from Romans where Paul states that justification is:

Romans 3:24	by His grace
Romans 4:24-25	in Jesus' resurrection
Romans 5:1	by faith
Romans 5:9	by His blood
Romans 8:33	by God

Add to the list James 2:24, "You see then that a man is justified by works, and not by faith only," and one can correctly conclude that Christians are justified by grace, by Jesus' resurrection, by faith, by His blood, by God and by works. If it is true that James contradicts Paul, then isn't it also true that Paul contradicts himself on a number of occasions? The obvious truth is that all of these are correct.

"The alleged difficulties in this section are not of the inspired writer's making." [33] Moses Lard accurately explains the situation when he wrote:

> [T]he doctrine of justification and the doctrine of remission of sins are identical doctrines. A man can not be justified, and his sins remain unforgiven; nor be forgiven, and remain unjustified. Now it is held by all who have a proper regard for the Bible, that no one can be forgiven without repentance. Further: it is conceded by all, that repentance is one act of obedience to Christ's authority, and belief a different act. These two acts can never be confounded; nor has the one any power either to usurp the place of the other, or to supplant it. Each performs a special function which the other can not perform; nor can either become a substitute for the other. How now, in the light of this, can belief be the sole condition of justification? The truth is, it is impossible. [34]

James, Paul and Jesus all taught the same thing regarding faith. Saving faith is living, active and obedient. "We are not saved by deeds; we are saved for deeds." [35]

James' letter has a long history of controversy simply because of the all-too-human tendency of trying to force God's Word to conform to one's preconceived beliefs. This is ultimately a failure to recognize the Bible as God's Word, the standard to which all disciples must humbly conform in obedience to Christ. May this generation learn from the mistakes of the past, not repeat them.

STUDY QUESTIONS

1. Describe the Hieronymian view of authorship.

2. What is the significance of the word "cousin" as it relates to James?

3. In what way was James an apostle?

4. What is the Helvidius view of authorship?

5. What is the Epiphanian view of authorship?

6. What resulted from Luther's "tower experience"?

7. Explain Luther's approach to Bible study leading up to his rejection of James.

8. What imagery did Luther apply from 1 Corinthians 3:12-13 to James?

9. What did Luther do to Romans 3:28 to support his ideas?

10. How can Romans 3:28 and James 2:24 be harmonized?

CHAPTER 7

THE *Face* OF FAITH

(JAMES 2:14-26)

Imagine the frustration of the Council Bluff, Iowa, family who, in making preparations for an overseas trip, were refused a passport for their 11-year-old son. County and state government offices had no official record of the child's birth. According to the government, the boy did not exist.[1] After looking at the child, the authorities could hardly dispute that he was real. But there was an obvious lack of agreement between their official records and the physical evidence.

The profession of true religion, as defined by James, must agree with the proper evidence of a spiritual birth (e.g. baptism, Acts 2:38; 22:16; James 1:18) followed by a living faith (v. 21). The pure religion God accepts is enlivened by an obedient, working faith (vv. 22, 27).

As discussed in Chapter 6, James 2:14-26 has been the source of controversy for years. At the center of the storm was Martin Luther, who was convinced that he found a clear contradiction between James and Paul. Although he agreed with James when he wrote, "Faith is a living, daring confidence in God's grace … so it is impossible for it not to do good works incessantly," [2] Luther cast a shadow of doubt over who God had chosen (James 2:5). James, however, did not disagree with Paul. Both urged only a living, obedient faith (1:22).

But one can have a faith that consists only of words (James 2:14-17). Many trace President George H.W. Bush's failed re-election campaign effort to his bold and emphatic statement, "Read my lips: no new taxes." Subsequent political decisions placed him in a position that allowed his opponents to portray him as having broken his word. At least in part, Bush's loss came because many were convinced that his words didn't match his actions. That disturbing gap between saying and doing is the subject addressed by James. The prejudice revealed in James 2 revealed a failure of some to practice the royal law they preached. Confronted with their hypocrisy, the church was quick to respond, "Read our lips … ." Their faith was only a verbal faith. James illustrates this superficial faith with another example (vv. 2-3). How does this faith respond in the face of a need?

FAITH WITHOUT WORKS

Two straightforward questions open this passage. The first is, "What does it profit, my brethren, if someone says he has faith but does not have works?" (James 2:14). His tone is softened by the tender address, "my brethren," even while his aggressive argumentation is driven forward by this probing question, testing the validity of one's professed faith. What is the advantage of a lifeless faith? Proponents of the "faith only" position argue that this individual only claims to have faith ("if someone says") but was never an actual believer. Yet, James doesn't question one's faith, only its active nature. Although James recognizes the possibility of an inactive faith, he quickly insists that it must not be tolerated.

James' second question is, "Can faith save him?" (James 2:14). The faith under consideration is inactive and can be expressed only in words. Can that kind of faith save? James clearly teaches that it cannot. One's words reveal a faith that incessantly asserts it is present but shows no sign of life. James is not saying persons can earn their way into heaven, only that true faith is active. In this he agrees perfectly with Paul (Romans 2:6; 6:13, 16).

Tightrope walker Jean Francois Gravelot, "The Great Blondin," once crossed a wire stretched over the Niagara River. He then asked the crowd, "Do you believe that I can push this wheelbarrow over?" They nodded enthusiastically. When he asked for a volunteer to ride in the wheelbarrow, no one would accept his offer.[3] Saving faith is evident only by the visible actions of trusting obedience. James warns the saved not to rely on a faith of words alone.

To illustrate, James draws attention to the condition of the poor fellow believer hypothetically in their presence who is described as "naked and destitute of daily food" (James 2:15), "a condition of want that would touch the hearts of all but the hardest." [4] "Naked" does not necessarily mean nude; it can also refer to one who is not properly or adequately clothed.[5] Whether ill-clad or unclad, his need is great and pressing. So how will a faith that has no works respond?

An imaginary speaker steps forward to represent the "faith without works" group, saying, "Depart in peace, be warmed and filled" (James 2:16). With words that make it sound as if real concern is present between them, the needy is dismissed without his or her needs met while the well-dressed man turns away in self-satisfaction as if he had met each of the pressing needs of his unfortunate brother. Rather than looking out for those in need (1:27), the inactive faith is content with lofty words and empty sentiment, leaving the helpless to fend for themselves.

Again James poses the question, "[W]hat does it profit," or what is the value of empty blessings (James 2:16b)? "The preposterousness of such a command is no doubt intentional. 'What good is it?' James asks. Its seeming concern for the welfare of the poor person is a worthless facade." [6] Their words convey concern, but their actions do not benefit the needy. The influence of the One who depicted the final judgment with images of sharing one's goods in His name (Matthew 25:37-40) is evident in James' words. Saving faith must have works. "One is not warmed by good wishes; one cannot fill an empty stomach with greetings." [7]

A faith that produces only words benefits no one; it is dead (James 2:17). James answers the question of whether the hypothetical believer he has been discussing possessed a real faith. Behind the words, the verbal profession of faith, is a real faith not practiced in real life; it is therefore dead. James Burton Coffman explains: "Is a dead body no longer a body? Is a dead body not real? Is a dead body different in nature from a living body?" So is this faith real faith not properly practiced. "The most marvelous body that ever lived may be compared with the most marvelous faith that ever existed; but if that marvelous faith is without works, it then has the same status as a dead corpse." [8] Without the necessary works (i.e., evidence of its life and productivity), that faith is dead and useless.

"YOU HAVE FAITH; I HAVE DEEDS"

One can have faith as a mental discipline (James 2:18-20). James uses a common expression, "[S]omeone may well say" (NASB), to introduce a new speaker who offers an alternate viewpoint (Romans 9:19; 11:19; 1 Corinthians 15:35). In this case James imagines an objection to his illustration and offers a hypothetical argument defending the inactive believer (James 2:18). To state the argument only illustrates its absurdity as these verses pose an impossible challenge for supporters of the "faith only" doctrine.

To prove that faith and works are not independent of each other, James imagines that they are and supposes that one person has faith and another has deeds. With these two imaginary believers, he presents the challenge: "Show me your faith without deeds." The only way faith can be demonstrated is through actions – works. One Christian cannot specialize exclusively in "believing" and another in "acting." James is arguing that even the "faith only" people must have action to prove their faith is present.

James states that to have a faith in thought only is to believe like the demons (James 2:19; Mark 1:34). This faith also must be rejected as useless (James 2:20). It is insufficient simply to recognize a basic belief in the unity of God and the Godhead. Twice every day, and often in the synagogues, this fundamental Jewish doctrine from Deuteronomy 6:4 – "The Lord our God, the Lord is one" – was recited.[9] James was quick to recognize the value of such a confession. To possess a faith that reveals a clear understanding of God is to "do well." That kind of faith has an alluring quality of goodness.[10] Their understanding is clear and correct up to the point of giving mental agreement to God's truth. But James says that such a faith cannot be distinguished from the faith of demons.

Three items are important to note about the demons (Greek *daimonion*). First, their precise identity is uncertain. The term sometimes refers to evil spirits of a lower rank than Satan himself, idols (Acts 17:18), fallen angels (Matthew 25:41; Revelation 12:7-8), ministers of Satan (Luke 4:35; John 10:21), and as a title for Satan (Matthew 9:34; Mark 3:22; Luke 11:15).[11] Second, these demons possessed a real faith in God, which is evident in their recognition of Jesus as God's Son (Matthew 8:28-32; Mark 1:23-26). Unfortunately, the third significant point is that the chance to repent and be reinstated to God's faithful service is no longer available to them. Therefore, their only response is to "tremble" – all they can do at the thought of their eternal punishment is shake in terror. For faith to hold the promise of eternal salvation, it must progress beyond thoughts and words to express itself in one's daily life.

THE FAITH OF ABRAHAM

James again draws his inevitable conclusion that "faith without works is dead" (James 2:20b; cf. vv. 14, 17). He begins by calling his audience back to a true, active faith in Christ. In his words, "But do you want to know, O foolish man," James issues a plea for those who possess an inactive faith to recognize the error of their position and join him on the solid ground of truth.[12] The "foolish man" is actually empty-headed, vain and described as "devoid of spiritual understanding." [13] Such is the state of any who attempt to establish the validity of faith without the supporting evidence of good works. Faith and works are not an either/or proposition. Both are required, just as inhaling requires exhaling. Without both working together, death will result.

Saving faith is an active force (James 2:21-24). Saving faith is more than just words. When a need is recognized, true faith responds with a willingness to act in meeting that need. More than mere mental agreement to the basics of religion, true faith demonstrates itself in obeying God's commands (Matthew 7:19-23). Abraham is an example of such faith. James called Abraham "our father," a fact many take as proof that he wrote to Christian Jews. However, Paul, the apostle to the Gentiles (Romans 11:13), spoke of Abraham in this manner (Galatians 3:7). James recognized Abraham's example as the father of the faithful whether formerly Jewish or Gentile. From the time he was called until his death, he exhibited an obedient faith (Genesis 12–25:11), but especially in his willingness to offer Isaac (James 2:21-22).

James specifically states that Abraham was justified. God proclaimed Abraham innocent when he offered Isaac because he acted out of obedience to God's direct command (Genesis 22:1-2). Abraham enjoyed divine approval before offering Isaac, but this is simply one example (no doubt the most dramatic) of his obedient faith responding in a visible work.

James used the same language and texts as Paul, illustrating that both agreed about the faith and justification of this great patriarch (Romans 4:3). Abraham's faith was genuine because it "was working together," cooperating "with his works" (James 2:22). It was that cooperation between faith and works that illustrates the true nature of faith. Because of the impact sin makes on an individual's life, there "is no case of 'pure' justification. No man ever existed who was justified without something else happening at the same time." [14] Faith must obey, a response that enables it to become perfect or mature (James 2:22).

Three things resulted from Abraham's obedience: he demonstrated his willingness to obey; he pleased God; and although an imperfect mortal, he was considered righteous. Abraham was technically not righteous (Ecclesiastes 7:20), but God credited him with righteousness on the basis of his faith when he obeyed God's command (Ezra 9:13). As a result, God's pleasure is expressed by calling Abraham "the friend of God" (James 2:23; cf. 2 Chronicles 20:7; Isaiah 41:8). James drives home his familiar conclusion (James 2:24). This is the only place in the New Testament where the words "faith only" are found together, and they deny rather than support the modern "faith only" position.

THE FAITH OF RAHAB

Rahab is James' final example of living faith. A Gentile harlot is in stark contrast to Abraham, but she exemplifies true faith even from the lowest rung of the social ladder (James 2:25; Joshua 2). Both Abraham and Rahab "performed works which in themselves would have been illegal or sinful, unless they were undertaken in direct consequence of being understood as the will of God. In the instance of Rahab, it is likewise clear that in her case also, she was justified as a consequence of what she did, and not upon the basis of 'faith alone.'" [15]

Much has been written of Rahab as a Jericho harlot. Josephus tried to soften her image "by depicting her as simply an innkeeper." [16] Others conclude that her interaction with the Hebrew spies led to a conversion in faith and career because Rahab could not be justified and remain a harlot.[17] One Jewish tradition contends that she became Joshua's wife and was an ancestor of the prophets Jeremiah and Ezekiel.[18] Another suggests that she became the wife of Salmon (perhaps one of the spies). Their son was Boaz, husband of Ruth and grandfather of Jesse (Matthew 1:5).[19]

For his purposes, James recognizes that Rahab literally risked her life in becoming allied with the Israelites. She extended hope to all because even this unlikely woman embodied true faith. Rahab once again reinforces James' conclusion (James 2:26; cf. also vv. 14, 17, 20). Through Rahab, James accomplishes two vital goals: he establishes works as the "acid test" of true faith, and he proves that the faith/works principle "has universal application, embracing both patriarch and prostitute." [20] James again reminds his readers, "[F]aith without works is dead also" (2:26). Mortal man can never really escape the fact of death, defined by James as the separation of the body from the spirit that animates it (4:14). Once this happens, the body is no longer productive.

On Jesus' visit to Capernaum near the beginning of His public ministry, four men brought their invalid friend to Him for healing. When their way was repeatedly blocked, the men decided to take drastic measures and lower the man through the roof. Mark 2:5 says that Jesus "saw their faith." How did He see their faith? The very same way He and the world sees, or fails to see, the faith professed by Christians in the modern world – through works. That is what the face of faith looks like. "Do all the good you can, by all the means you can, in all the ways you can, in all the places you can, at all the times you can, to all the people you can, as long as ever you can." [21]

STUDY QUESTIONS

1. What kind of faith cannot save?

2. What example does James use of this?

3. How does James describe dead faith?

4. How does James say faith is revealed?

5. To what example of "faith only" does James refer in the spiritual realm?

6. How does James sum up this type of faith?

7. What examples are cited to describe true faith?

8. How is Abraham an example of faith?

9. How is Rahab an example of faith?

10. How does physical death relate to a dead faith?

CHAPTER 8

Sparks AND STORMS

(JAMES 3:1-12)

Every generation embraces its own fads, something unique everyone can do to express individuality (and to fit in with the crowd). Recent years have witnessed the popularity of body piercing. Consider the case of a Connecticut woman who was treated at Yale University's School of Medicine for a brain abscess caused by an infection from her recent tongue piercing. Both the American Dental Association and the American Academy of Dermatology issued a subsequent warning about the danger posed by the practice.[1] This came more than 1,900 years after James warned of a connection between the tongue and a "poisoned" mind.

THOSE WHO TEACH

The third chapter of James begins with a special emphasis on the role of Christian teachers. In James' day the church did not have access to the complete writings of the New Testament. Christians relied on the accuracy of their teachers. Against this backdrop, James returns to the topic of the tongue (cf. James 1:19, 26). His concern brings out a corrective tone in the gentle phrase, "my brethren" (3:1). Unlike those to whom Hebrews was addressed, James' audience aspired to fill the role of the Christian teacher (Hebrews 5:12). The force of James' statement in the original language takes the form of a command to stop a current practice.[2] The danger to the audience came in their allowing the unqualified to serve in this capacity (1 Timothy 1:7) or in aspiring to teach out of improper motives. Those seeking the role of Christian teacher for the glory or public show that accompanied that work must take pause to consider carefully the responsibility they are undertaking.

It is no wonder that James warns the church to stop the practice of allowing just anyone to teach. The position of the Christian teacher is essential, and the need for developing effective teachers in God's kingdom cannot be over emphasized. Yet, teachers must recognize the serious nature of the ministry and their increased responsibility ("a stricter judgment," James 3:1). All will be judged by the same standard (John 12:48), but the teacher will be judged more intensely: by the truth taught and the truth lived. The church must be selective in choosing its teachers.

CONTROLLING THE TONGUE

Teachers must take their ministry seriously because of their own struggle with sin (James 3:2; cf. Romans 3:23). Sin is universal. James includes himself when he writes that everyone stumbles over many things (i.e. different kinds of sin). Chief among the kinds of sin confronting the Christian are those involving the tongue. "It voices every evil feeling and every kind of sinful thought; it sets in motion and gives concreteness to every kind of sinful act." [3] The issue for James, as it relates to teachers, appears to be one of credibility. Because teachers fulfill their ministry by speaking, they are especially vulnerable to human criticism and divine judgment for failing to control their tongues in all settings. So James hopes to find teachers who, when warned of the risks involved, are still willing to discharge faithfully the ministry of teaching God's Word.

Because the tongue plays a key role in most sins, James argues that the person who masters his tongue is "a perfect man" in the sense of becoming mature or full grown (James 3:2; cf. 1:4; Matthew 5:48). If one is able to succeed in controlling the tongue, which is admittedly difficult to do (12:36), it can be assumed that he or she is succeeding also in disciplining the less obstinate members of the body (James 3:2).

All Christians need to be aware of the tongue's power and strive to control it (James 3:3-4). "Just as an old-fashioned doctor examined a patient's tongue to assist in diagnosis, so James tests a person's spiritual health by his or her conversation. Self-diagnosis begins with sins of speech." [4]

The power of the tongue is first illustrated and tied to the previous discussion in James 1:26 through the picture of a bridled horse (3:3). In James' day, the horse was not as common, especially in Palestine, as it is today. Usually associated with the Roman army in battle armor and with an armed soldier sitting astride it, the horse was a powerful figure. Among these trappings are the relatively tiny bridle encircling its head and the even smaller bit that the bridle holds in the horse's mouth. That tiny bit enables the rider to control the powerful animal. Just as the "body of the horse follows his mouth, guided by the bridle," [5] so the tongue, small as it is, directs the entire human body.

The second illustration comes from "the largest inanimate object that James's contemporaries might attempt to steer," [6] a cargo ship. Like his previous illustration, James compares the tiny rudder to the massive ship it guides. He also incorporates into this illustration other elements relating to the need to control one's tongue.

The tongue is difficult to control because it is driven by fierce passions as the ship is "driven by fierce winds" (James 3:4). The tongue is a tool employed to express these emotions. Behind the words are the unseen, hidden motives and desires of one's heart (Mark 7:20-23). The ship has an individual with his hand on the rudder, seeking to direct it even through "the fierce winds" of passion. The worldly desires behind the misuse of the tongue are countered by the spiritual desires of the one trying to control the tongue. So the "intention of the steersman lies back of the impact of the hand on the rudder." [7] The pilot's desires can turn the ship, guiding it to the chosen destination.

In his first two illustrations of the controlled tongue, James urges his readers not to underestimate the power of the tongue because of its size. Although it is a little member of the human body, the tongue "boasts great things" (James 3:5). With this statement James turns to his third illustration, this one showing the power of the uncontrolled tongue in producing evil. The real danger posed by the tongue is not in making the boasts but in its ability to fulfill them. "The tongue is able to sway multitudes. It can alter the destinies of nations" [8] (cf. Proverbs 18:21). In that realization James issues this memorable warning, "See how great a forest a little fire kindles!" (James 3:5b). Just one spark under certain conditions can ignite a devastating fire that destroys everything in its path. He paints a bold picture of the uncontrolled tongue's power to destroy. As a great fire, the uncontrolled tongue creates untold destruction (Psalms 52:2; 140:3; Proverbs 6:19; 12:18; 16:27-28; 26:28). The Great Chicago Fire of 1871, which urban legend states was started when Mrs. O'Leary's cow kicked over a lantern, "killed 250 people, made 100,000 homeless, and destroyed property valued at $175,000,000." [9] Burning like a wildfire, the tongue brings nothing but unhappiness and heartache into one's life.

James calls these problems "a world of iniquity" (James 3:6). The word "world" is used in the sense of "a mass, a great collection, an abundance." [10] Without the guidelines of godliness, "impure speech may take a multitude of forms." [11] The life fills then overflows with sin (cf. 1:21). The tiny tongue is capable of corrupting the entire body, the very thing James warned against in 1:27. The misuse of one's tongue can lead to the loss of his soul in hell (Matthew 12:37; 15:18).

Compounding the problems will be the negative impact his speech will have in the lives of others. The uncontrolled tongue not only brings unhappiness into the life of the speaker; it also touches the lives of innocent bystanders. Perhaps this perpetuation of hurt is what James has in mind in his phrase, "sets on fire the course of nature" (literally "the wheel of existence" or "wheel of human origin," James 3:6). This difficult phrase has been interpreted as reincarnation, the Greek torture wheel, [12] the circulatory system (Ecclesiastes 12:6), and "the successive generations of men ... through all the ages." [13] The most likely interpretation is "the time span of one's life," [14] with the "wheel" being set in motion at one's birth. This fits the context of James, who "emphasizes the effect of the tongue upon the person himself." [15] James is simply establishing the harmful effects that follow the Christian's failure to control the tongue.

Through his effective illustrations, James shows "that everything around man seems affected by the tongue." [16] Like the ripples on a pond when a pebble hits its surface, the "corrupting influence of the tongue reaches out in widening circles, for it 'sets the whole course of ... life on fire.' " [17] F.F. Bruce described it as fire spreading on a wheel from the axle hub "outward along the spokes and sets the whole wheel afire; so the mischief engendered by an irresponsible tongue can inflame human relationships and cause irreparable destruction."[18] It affects them and all of their relationships, even with God and Satan.

This assertion in James 3:6 undoubtedly captured the attention of James' readers, who would have never wanted to serve the devil. Yet, by failing to exercise control over their tongues, they are again in league with the devil, their tongues having been "set on fire by hell" (v. 6). James uses the word *gehenna* for hell. This is the only New Testament usage of that Greek word outside of the gospels. The unseen hand in control of their tongues is Satan himself.

TAMING THE TONGUE

James concludes that there is really no such thing as the "uncontrolled tongue." Any tongue not brought into subjection to heaven is effectively controlled by hell. Knowing this potential danger, James instructs his readers in the process of bringing the tongue under proper control. Make no mistake, it is no simple venture, but the benefits are well worth the effort. He reminds them that, from the earliest time, humanity has enjoyed superiority over all classes of created animals (Genesis 1:28; 9:2). James lists four kinds of created beings: beast (four-footed animals), birds, reptiles and fish (James 3:7). He is not saying that all types have been domesticated, only that mankind has been successful in bringing them all under control. However, man has not had success when it comes to taming the tongue, and he will not (v. 8).

James argues that without God's help success is unattainable. As Christians move toward spiritual maturity, they are expected to grow in their ability to control their speech. While the tongue cannot be permanently tamed, it can and must be controlled. Each individual is accountable for the use and abuse of his or her tongue.

Two traits, listed in James 3:8, make the tongue especially difficult to control. The first is its restlessness ("an unruly evil"). Just as Peter pictures the devil, so James describes the tongue as always pacing, readily available for use (1 Peter 5:8; James 3:6, 8). The Jewish rabbis, explaining Psalm 120:3, described God's rationale for His placement of the tongue in the human body: "God said to the tongue: All the rest of the members of the body are erect, but thou liest down; all the rest are external, but thou art internal. Nor is this enough: I have built two walls about thee; the one bone, the other flesh." [19] From the earliest time, the impromptu nature of the tongue, its constant ability to surprise and shame, has been recognized. The second trait is the tongue's capacity to hurt ("full of deadly poison"; James 3:8b; Psalms 58:3-4; 140:3; Romans 3:13-14). James rejects the "sticks and stones" philosophy. Words can poison the heart and life of the speaker while bringing lasting pain into the lives of others.

PRAISING AND CURSING

Chief Superintendent Moshe Karadi had been cracking down on speeders in Israel for months. One particular speeder Chief Karadi stopped was David Gaz, who ironically happened to be commander of traffic police in southern Israel. Needless to say, Gaz found himself unemployed. [20] The world has no problem recognizing the dangers of inconsistencies, so they should be able to understand the dangers James addresses when he turns to the inconsistency of uncontrolled speech (James 3:9-12).

James' concern is with those who speak adoringly of God in worship only to become consumed by bitter infighting after the close of services (James 4:1). "[M]any who, while they pretend to sing the high praises of God, are ready to wish the direst imprecations either on those who offend them, or with whom they choose to be offended." [21] The inconsistency is highlighted as James contrasts the "blessing and cursing" of his readers (3:9-10). They praise God only to turn around to curse those created in His image (1 John 4:20-21).

With both blessing and cursing springing from the same source, serious doubt arises over the true nature of that source. A blessing that comes from a corrupted source is itself corrupted.[22] This prompts James to remark, "[T]hese things ought not to be so" (James 3:10). "His phrase is rather like our 'It's not right!' spoken with all the force of protesting condemnation." [23]

Christians must strive to be pure in heart, a trait most clearly evident in their words. To be divided in one's mind (cf. James 1:8) is not only uncharacteristic of Christianity but also of creation itself. Drawing from common natural phenomenon, James proves that consistency is the rule, not the exception. Of the many springs in Palestine, some produced salty, undrinkable water, a few produced fresh water, but none produced both.[24] The source always produces water consistent with its own nature, so the tongue reveals the true content and nature of the heart.

Just how powerful is the tongue? It is so powerful it can void pure religion (James 1:26), satisfy a weak and dying faith (2:16), and divide brethren (4:11). James' real message is that the Christian can, in submitting to Jesus Christ and His commands, learn to control the tongue. The only conclusion consistent with the fact is that "these things ought not to be so" (3:10), indicating that it is possible for one to avoid this inconsistency, rather than "it's just part of being human and beyond your control."[25] Controlling the tongue is possible, James insists, but the individual Christian alone will never succeed (3:8). The victory rests only in Jesus.

In some segments of modern society, the emerging fad is to have the center of one's tongue split, making a "forked tongue" appearance. The state of Illinois proposed legislation to monitor strictly those who perform this "service."[26] They are worried about infection and the effects on one's body. But James' chief concern about the tongue is with the heart and soul of each Christian, who he insists has the ability, in Christ, to use the gift of speech to bring glory to God and the gospel to the lost.

STUDY QUESTIONS

1. Why does James address teachers in 3:1?

2. What are the implications of one's success in controlling the tongue?

3. What two examples are used about the controlled tongue?

4. What example is used about the uncontrolled tongue?

5. Explain the phrase "world of iniquity."

6. Explain the phrase "course of nature."

7. Explain the phrase "set on fire by hell."

8. Explain the distinction between taming and controlling the tongue.

9. Explain the phrases "unruly evil" and "deadly poison."

10. How are the inconsistencies of the tongue depicted?

CHAPTER 9

Words OF WISDOM

(JAMES 3:13-18)

In the never-ending quest to maintain control of one's tongue, James' conviction is obvious: the task is impossible without God's help. Wisdom, essential for purity in speech (Colossians 4:5-6), is freely available to those willing to approach God submissively in faith (James 1:5). In fact, God is eager to give this vital gift to His children (1:17). James follows his presentation on the need to control one's tongue (3:1-12) with a discussion of the type of wisdom the task requires.

While knowledge, the collecting of facts and information, is vital in both the social and religious worlds, learning alone offers no benefit toward the proper control of the tongue. The world has seen its share of brilliant individuals. Thomas Edison was the greatest inventor of all time. He is credited with more than 1,000 patents and is responsible for many of the common appliances and electronic gadgets in modern homes. He modestly attributed his success to persistence rather then intellect, saying, "Genius is one percent inspiration, ninety-nine percent perspiration." [1] Edison was an expert at adapting his vast scientific knowledge to practical uses.

Edison's fellow scientist Albert Einstein became a dominant figure in the field of physics, being awarded the Nobel Prize in 1921. In 1939 Einstein wrote to President Franklin Roosevelt that Hitler might develop an atomic bomb. His warning prompted research leading to the ultimate victory over the evil dictator and his allies. Today Einstein's name is equated with intellectual superiority, or the lack thereof, as in "he is no Einstein."

But no amount of knowledge adequately replaces true spiritual wisdom. "Knowledge is proud that she has learned so much, Wisdom is humble that she knows no more." [2] According to James, wisdom is essential to spiritual success. The Greek word for wisdom appears to have been derived from the Hebrew word for watchman, the one who sees the danger approach outside the city walls and warns the citizens inside. To be wise is to be properly informed and moved to appropriate action. Wisdom gathers information and then skillfully makes proper application of that information. James 3:13-18 contains a careful examination of wisdom.

"Who is wise and understanding among you?" (James 3:13). With this question it appears that James is alluding to the teachers of 3:1. The plight of unqualified teachers is most clearly demonstrated by the lack of wisdom. Perhaps attracted by the prestige and honor they attach to the role of public teaching, they advanced themselves as "wise," a "technical term among the Jews for the teacher, the scribe, the rabbi." [3] It was worn like a religious title. The word "understanding" described "an expert, the skilled and scientific person with a tone of superiority." [4] The poor teachers are quick to cite their qualifications, claiming to be experts. James will expose the motives and values of both the worldly wise and truly wise while giving motivation to those seeking heavenly wisdom to continue their noble quest. Clearly more is demanded of Christian teachers than just the possession of and ability to teach the facts relating to the faith.

Wisdom, like faith, is displayed in attitudes and deeds (James 2:18; 3:13). Knowledge is shown in words, ideas, concepts and formulas. A scholar may be able to relate the meaning, history, development and implications of the Greek word *agape* without exhibiting its characteristics in his daily life. Wisdom is living knowledge (1:22; 2:17; 4:17). While teachers necessarily work with words, James calls for evidence that the truths taught are practiced in their lives. The phrase "[l]et him show" (3:13) calls for proof that must come in actions. "Actions speak louder than words even in the case of the professional wise man" [5] (cf. 1 Peter 1:15).

Wisdom is also gentle or meek (James 3:13b). The meek are in complete control of their emotions and interactions with others. Meekness "is not passivity, or weakness, but strength under control. It is the opposite of arrogance, which demands that superiority be recognized." [6] Even here the teacher and student are equals (cf. 1:21). The humble individual is receptive and obedient to God's Word, two qualities of the most effective Christian teacher.

SEVEN TRAITS OF EARTHLY WISDOM

At the heart of this passage rests the warning of two different kinds of wisdom. "Just as there are wicked and righteous uses of the tongue, so there are demonic and divine manifestations of wisdom (James 3:13–18). James contrasts seven characteristics of human wisdom with seven qualities of divine wisdom." [7] In describing wisdom, James incorporates the sad circumstances of his readers, achieved through the human wisdom of their teachers' bitter jealousy and selfish ambition, arrogance, disorder and evil (3:14-16; 4:1) with the fruit of true, spiritual wisdom. The only goal of human wisdom is pleasing and advancing the interests of the individual (3:14-16). Seven traits are clearly identifiable in James' description of this personification of earthly wisdom. At every turn, he provides a glimpse into the selfishness and worldliness that empowers human wisdom. The list, like false wisdom itself, descends until its insidious origin is clearly identifiable.

1. Envy. The English word "zeal" comes directly from this Greek word meaning desire. Being neutral, its context determines if that desire is envy or zeal. In this case, the word "bitter" clearly reveals James' negative use of the word (James 3:14; see also Ephesians 4:31). His phrasing verifies that this was the current status of his original audience.[8] Their attitude was harmful to Christian fellowship and contrary to the Christian message itself.

2. Self-seeking. A self-absorbed attitude is the companion of envy. James used a word that describes a "self-centered and self-serving ambition." [9] Arndt and Gingrich say that its only known occurrence prior to the New Testament was in "Aristotle where it denotes a self-seeking pursuit of political office by unfair means." [10] The self-seeking teacher's driving passion "is to advance his own interests," [11] to gain "advantage and prestige." [12] These negative traits spring from a sin-darkened heart (Matthew 15:18-19).

3. Boasting. Unqualified teachers are an arrogant group. To them it is not an honor to teach; it is the student's honor to sit at their feet. They frequently remind their students just how lucky they are to learn under such wonderful instructors. Their self-flattering words and the life they lead often contradict the message they teach. "Boasting arrogance disproves the possession of wisdom." [13]

4. Lie against the truth. James depicts boasting as a lie against the truth because it contradicts the clear teaching of Scripture. His phrasing describes a current practice where teachers are taking "a harsh stance of demanding to be recognized as wise, instead of being willing to learn." [14] James commands them to stop. His warning is a strong reminder of their duty to live the truth they teach.

5. Earthly. The wisdom James has been discussing (earthly wisdom) is distinct from the wisdom he is encouraging. It is a boast rather than God's gift (James 1:17). It did not come from God and "isn't godly, [but is] a wisdom of this world; 1 Cor. 1:20,21; 2:4-6; 3:19; 2 Cor. 1:12." [15] This false wisdom is of the earth and fails even to consider possible or potential life above. These "wise" individuals can never fully appreciate God's truth.

6. Sensual. Not only is false wisdom "of the earth"; it appeals to the carnal aspect of the teacher's prideful nature. James uses a word that literally means "animal-like." For the false teachers, the spiritual takes a back seat to the sensual. This wisdom is only an imposter; it is not spiritual in nature. It did not find its origin with God and will never lead anyone to Him.

7. Demonic. James forever links false wisdom with hell itself. It is "demon-like," a word that appears only here in the New Testament. [16] Rather than originating in heaven, it comes from hell. "His investigation of false wisdom uncovers the same source as his investigation of the uncontrolled tongue in 3:6 – they are both from hell." [17] The sinfulness of this false wisdom is clearly demonstrated by James' portrayal of it in these verses. He shows the infectious nature of sin as the "adjectives build upon each other in an ascending scale of wickedness" [18] and a strikingly intentional "downward progression": earthly; sensual; demonic. [19]

Having outlined the traits of false wisdom, James now briefly describes its unhappy results (James 3:16). "One sin begets another, and it cannot be imagined how much mischief is produced."[20] The product of earthly wisdom is described as a harvest, but not as fruit. Rather, James heaps together a collection of negative words indicating the terrible results suffered by those who embrace this mentality. In an environment of "envy and self-seeking" (v. 14), one can only expect a negative harvest. The ruins of earthly wisdom, as listed by James, are "confusion and every evil thing" (v. 16b). The word "confusion" means, "tumultuous anarchy,"[21] and is contrary to God's will (1 Corinthians 14:33; 2 Corinthians 12:20). James then sweeps into this sentence "[every] worthless, vile, wicked, base and good-for-nothing thing."[22] Such is always the result when sin reigns, and it is especially tragic when it describes the life of the Christian teacher. James traces such an individual's "self-destruction" from envy downward as sin leads to more sin until earthly wisdom has finally exacted its full price.

SEVEN TRAITS OF HEAVENLY WISDOM

Livermore, Calif., is a "city that prides itself as a center of advanced science." So it was only fitting to hire an artist to paint a mosaic outside the city library commemorating society's great intellectuals, such as "William Shakespere and Albert Eistien." After spending $40,000 for the mosaic, city officials discovered that it contained the misspelled names of those they intended to honor.[23]

The imperfections of worldly wisdom are brought into sharp contrast as James paints a portrait of true, heavenly wisdom (James 3:17-18). True wisdom is from God, the Giver of perfect gifts (1:17), and it seeks to serve others while obeying Him. The caution of Burton Coffman is timely: "This does not mean that mortals are directly inspired by such wisdom, but that God is the ultimate source from which their wisdom is actually received." He also points out that, although James does not divulge "the means of their receiving it," the only possible source of this wisdom, compatible with the Scriptures, is the sincere study of the Scriptures themselves. James gives seven traits to describe this heavenly wisdom.[24]

1. Pure. James says it is "first pure" (James 3:17). The word "first" points to the basic characteristic of heavenly wisdom, the one trait from which all other traits depend.[25] Only when purity is in place can the other characteristics of true wisdom flourish in the believer's life.

True wisdom is pure, "free from iniquity and defilements, not allowing of any known sin, but studious of holiness both in heart and life."[26] From the word for "holy" and "saint," purity is a basic concept of the Christian faith and an immutable quality of God. "From this inner quality flow the outward manifestations given in the rest of the verse."[27] It is free from envy, strife and boasting.

2. Peaceable. Out of purity, peace will flourish. This is the quality of "[living] in peace with others, and promoting peace among men."[28] James exhibits wisdom by placing purity before peace because God's truth must be prized over peace. James often reminds the reader of Jesus' teaching in the Beatitudes (Matthew 5:9). Peace is contrasted with the envy and self-seeking of worldly wisdom previously discussed.

3. Gentle. A gentle person is humble, kind, "forbearing; making allowances for others,"[29] "[thoughtful] and respectful of other people's feelings."[30] Such a person makes every effort to "[put] the best construction upon all the actions of others."[31] Paul commended this quality, especially in Christian teachers (2 Timothy 2:24).

4. Willing to yield. Here James describes the quality of one "easily persuaded,"[32] "approachable,"[33] and "[willing] to listen to and obey others."[34] Without compromising the truth of God's Word, the Christian should be of such a nature that others feel at ease interacting with him. This is especially true for Christian teachers (Proverbs 9:8-9). The worldly wise couldn't appreciate this trait.

5. Full of mercy and good fruits. Unlike the every kind of evil produced by earthly wisdom (James 3:16), true wisdom produces Christlike compassion in the believer. In this phrase James describes the active quality of mercy: "always ready to help those who are in need."[35] This is the basis of the life filled with good works so often depicted by Paul (Ephesians 2:10; Philippians 1:11; Titus 3:1, 14).

6. Without partiality. Unlike the "double-minded man" of James 1:6-8, this word means, "fair and without deception, deceit, or fraud,"[36] "not acting one way in one circumstance and another in a different one." [37] As a teacher he will be "unwavering and uncompromising" [38] concerning God's Word.

7. Without hypocrisy. The final trait of heavenly wisdom is a word that means "sincere, unfeigned." [39] Hypocrisy was an attitude Jesus strongly condemned (Matthew 23). "This wisdom doesn't play-act. ... It does not deal in deception. ... It is not the wisdom which is clever at putting on disguises and concealing its real aims and motives." [40] There is nothing false about such teachers. Their main aim is to glorify God.

THE FRUITS OF WISDOM

James concludes his discussion of wisdom's traits with a brief description of its fruits (James 3:18). In a somewhat cumbersome verse, he describes righteousness as a crop. The necessary environment for it to thrive is peace (Romans 12:18; 14:19; Colossians 3:15; 2 Timothy 2:22; 1 Peter 3:11). When the seed (God's Word; Mark 4:14) is sown in peace, the conditions are excellent for righteousness to grow in the lives of God's people. Such a harvest is impossible in an environment of bitter envy and strife. The seed must be sown and the field properly tended. "The qualities in 3:17 don't just happen or naturally arise. Such wonderful traits must be taught and nurtured." [41]

Today his name is synonymous with intelligence, yet Albert Einstein reportedly said that during his lifetime he had two ideas.[42] James reminds his readers that God's gift is greater than anything human intellect could ever design. God gives sufficient wisdom to live the Christian life fully (1 John 5:3). "The fruit reaped by the planting of wisdom is a bountiful crop of righteousness." [43] One place it will be especially noticeable is in the spiritually maturing Christian's speech.

STUDY QUESTIONS

1. Define the terms "wise" and "understanding" (3:13).

2. How is true wisdom to be demonstrated?

3. What traits are used to describe earthly wisdom?

4. Describe the spiral effect evident in James 3:15-16.

5. What is the source of true wisdom?

6. What is the significance of the word "first" in James 3:17?

7. List and describe the traits of heavenly wisdom in verse 17.

8. Explain the imagery in verse 18.

9. Who "sows peace" in the world?

10. Contrast the harvests of the two kinds of wisdom.

CHAPTER 10

Wisdom AT WORK

(JAMES 4:1-10)

The ongoing turmoil in the Middle East prompted a plea from an animal rights activist group (PETA), who sent a letter to Yasser Arafat protesting the suicide bombings conducted by Palestinians in Israel. Specifically, they objected to a Jan. 26, 2003, bombing in which a donkey was used. When asked their views on bombings where no animals are employed, the PETA spokesperson responded, "It's not my business … to inject myself into human wars." [1]

Life is sacred. Senseless killing of any living being is wrong. Yet there is a distinction between the life of a human and that of a donkey. Like those whose confused values see animal and human life in different places than where they should be, Christians originally addressed by James had confused values. Brotherly love was replaced with civil war as the will of the strong was forced upon the weak. Having just contrasted the nature and danger of earthly wisdom with the qualities of true wisdom, James now turns to his readers' pressing need for heavenly wisdom (James 4:1-4).

All was not well for those to whom James originally wrote. As the fourth chapter of his epistle reveals, they were deeply entrenched in a serious war. Many of the Greek words used in these verses are the root words for familiar English words, such as *polemeo* for "wars" in verse 1 (English: "polemic"). Both terms, "wars" and "fights," indicate a level of hostility within the church. " 'War' implies continued hostility; 'battle' the occasional outburst." [2]

Some commentators argue that the conflict addressed in verse 1 is on a national level, the Jewish Wars. It seems clear, however, that James is speaking of a subject more directly under the influence of the individual Christian. At the most the conflict is congregational and at the least individual. He is considering the same battle that has been present from his opening words: the struggle to live consistently with one's faith. Lest one trivialize the seriousness of the situation, it should be remembered that heavenly wisdom produces peace, not wars and battles. The presence of these conflicts provides concrete evidence of the type of wisdom predominant among their membership.

THE STRUGGLE FOR PLEASURE

The source of the combative spirit is an overemphasis on pleasure (*hedone*; "hedonism"). The drive to satisfy their desire is the spark leading to their wars (*strateuo*; "strategy"), a conflict that is ongoing. James does not mean the members of the congregation, but rather their physical bodies. "Every conflict we have begins with us: in our bodies, in our minds, in our emotions." [3] While the visible battle is fought between fellow Christians, the real struggle is the war going on within the individual believer.

• **Covetousness.** The process of this struggle is carefully outlined in James 4:2. The word *epithumeo*, "lust," is best rendered "covet," an intense longing for the forbidden. The phrases "you covet" and "do not have" are in the present tense, indicating continuous action. James is saying, "You keep coveting for what you continue to not possess." [4] Their covetous thirst is insatiable, but that is the nature of covetousness; it alone is blind to its hopelessness.

Determined to succeed in a futile effort, they "murder and covet and cannot obtain" (James 4:2). His use of the term "murder" has led some to conclude that James is writing to a non-Christian audience or discussing conflict on a governmental level, higher than that of the church. This would be necessary only if James meant for the term "murder" to be taken literally. Christ, in His Sermon on the Mount, equated hatred with murder (Matthew 5:21-22; cf. 1 John 3:15). The usage here should be so understood. These people will stop at nothing to gain their coveted pleasure.

The present tense is used both for the hatred of those envied (Greek *epithumeo*, "yearning passion for") and for the desire itself (Greek *zeloute*, a form of the word *zelos*, from which the English word "zeal" is derived).[5] "The unfulfilled longing becomes so powerful that we trample on those who seem to obstruct our progress."[6] On one occasion the wealthy philanthropist John D. Rockefeller was asked, "How much money is enough money?" He replied, "Just a little bit more!"[7] Materialism and covetousness are impossible to satisfy. Even fueled with the heat of hatred, the desires of covetousness cannot be quenched. James' words "cannot obtain" are literally the negated form of the Greek word from which the word "dynamite" is derived. In this case it means that they do not have the power to acquire. So, James says, the war continues.

• **Prayer**. A new dimension is introduced at the end of verse two as James considers the role of prayer in the misguided quest to fulfill one's selfish desires. Could it be that the reason one's desires are unfulfilled is because they have not taken the matter before God in prayer? The reason they "do not have" is not just that they have not taken it up in prayer, begging God, but that their motives when they do pray are unacceptable. They constantly asked Him to grant their desires, but their prayers were not granted. "You ask and do not receive" (James 4:3a). "Why?" James wonders. "[B]ecause you ask amiss, that you may spend it on your pleasures" (v. 3b).

Their motives in prayer were misguided and sinful; they asked so they could waste it on a hedonistic lifestyle. So strong was their desire to do whatever felt good that they hated everyone who had what they wanted and those who seemed to be standing in their way of gaining the coveted pleasure.

• **Friendship With the World**. Although James has tenderly addressed his readers throughout as beloved brethren, in no way is he blind to the serious danger posed by sin. In recognition of this fact, he employs the strong language of verse 4. Sin hinders the Christian's development toward spiritual maturity. Left unchecked, the result is eternal death (Romans 6:23). These people are adulterers and adulteresses because, as the bride of Christ, they had fallen in love with the world (2 Corinthians 11:2; Romans 7:1-6; Revelations 21:2; 22:17). Loving the world de-emphasizes and actually prohibits a meaningful relationship with God. They no longer know that to align with the material world is to be opposed to God as His enemy. Friendship with the world "refers to a Christian's loving the pleasures, enticements and lusts of society in general, a friendship that tends inevitably to forsaking the Lord." [8]

It is impossible to maintain a friendship with the world and God at the same time. James warns that "if pleasure is the policy of life, then nothing but strife and hatred and division can possibly follow." [9] In the end it is the individual's choice. If they choose the world's values over Christ's, they will find themselves in a state of rebellion against God – spiritual adultery. They become His enemies. James emphasizes individual responsibility in the words "wants" and "makes." It is impossible to love God while continuing in sin's service (Matthew 6:24; 1 John 2:15). Although the practice of earthly wisdom produces only misery and heartache, James is anxious to show that wisdom from above can work in one's life.

THE SCRIPTURES AND THE SPIRIT

Many commentators have labeled James 4:5-6 the most difficult verses of Chapter 4. [10] James refers to "the Scripture" but fails to quote a specific passage. Some claim he intended only to offer a summary of the gist of scriptural teaching (Proverbs 3:34); others suggest he never intended to make a quotation. "[The] first sentence usually being presented as a formula for introducing a Scriptural quotation ... The proof that this does not introduce a quotation from the Bible is that no quotation is given, a problem which has perplexed the commentators extensively." [11]

James may be asking two rhetorical questions emphasizing the purity that always results from following the Holy Spirit. 1) Does the Scripture speak in vain? 2) Does the Holy Spirit within Christians envy things of the world? The idea is that when the Bible speaks it is accurate and that the Spirit never contributes to one's sin. "If one can be friends with both the church and the world, then what God has said in the Scriptures is in vain." [12] God's Word never says anything in vain (Isaiah 55:10-11). The crucial question then relates to the identification of "the spirit" (the human spirit or the Holy Spirit) and the source of the envy (God's or man's). While commentators present up to four alternate interpretations, only two appear to fit the intentions of the inspired writer.

• **The Human Spirit View.** One view is that the human spirit, given at creation (Genesis 2:7; James 2:26), has been corrupted by sin and now envies the things of the world (cf. 3:14). Some versions add a question mark to this verse, emphasizing that this spirit, when first given, did not envy. Furthermore, God has not left man to struggle alone, "He gives more grace or strength whenever it is needed (Heb. 4:16)." [13] This strength is available to every Christian through the non-miraculous measure of the Holy Spirit given at baptism (Acts 2:38; 5:32). As the hazards of life are braved, the Christian will find in God an "ever increasing grace" [14] from God, sufficient to do His Will, because of His love for them and His desire for their devotion and fellowship.

• **The Holy Spirit View.** Some think James referred to the Holy Spirit, which the Christian received at baptism, Who becomes "jealous" when the Christian grows too affectionate with the material world (NKJV). True to James' declaration of God's holiness in James 1:13, the Spirit is portrayed as longing for the Christian's complete devotion. [15] Like a loving husband betrayed by an adulterous wife, the Spirit is jealous when the believer loves the world. God offers more grace toward those willing to repent, making forgiveness a reality. "God will not take second place in our lives (Matthew 6:33). And God won't share our devotion with someone or something else (Matthew 6:24)." [16]

Both interpretations lead to the conclusion that God has made every provision possible for the individual faithfulness of every Christian. This alone is the path away from friendship with the world and toward friendship with God. He provides all the strength they need but allows them the complete freedom to choose. James calls his readers back to a careful study of and a conformation to the will of Christ evidenced by a living and active faith. Using Proverbs 3:34 in James 4:6, James shows that God stands opposed to those who are proud (refusing to repent) while showing grace to those who are "humble" (literally, "not rising far from the ground" [17]). God will not give anything to the proud, and their selfish prayers go unanswered (James 4:1-4). But to the humble, He draws near, giving grace.

SUBMITTING TO GOD

In James 4:7-10, fallen Christians are shown how to return to God in obedience. Such a response places them in submission to God (v. 7), a "Greek military term meaning 'to arrange [troop divisions] in a military fashion under the command of a leader.' In non-military use it referred to 'a voluntary attitude of giving in, cooperating, assuming responsibility, and carrying a burden.' " [18] This is a bold declaration of allegiance to God, which is met with specific promises from Him. Because God opposes the proud but helps the humble, believers should submit to Him. Submission is not the same as obedience, but in surrendering one's will to God they are placed in a position that makes obedience possible.

The Christian's submissive relationship to God involves an active, deliberate resistance of the devil. Although Satan is much more powerful than the individual Christian, he is far less powerful than God. Therefore, when a submissive believer is actively resisting the devil's efforts, the devil will flee. Here is the wonderful truth that "if a man takes a resolute stand against the devil, he will prove him a coward." [19]

An even greater promise is coupled with this one: as the Christian draws close to God, God reciprocates (James 4:8). God's divine nature requires certain prerequisites for the spiritual fellowship James describes. Some respected commentators object to the idea that James addresses these verses to believers because they are described as sinners. However, one must consider the specific commands James has already issued to his readers, charging them to stop blaming God when they are tempted (1:13), stop holding their faith with respect of persons (2:1), stop being arrogant, and stop lying against the truth (3:14). Even in this chapter James' readers are depicted as participating in wars, fights, envy, hatred and the pursuit of pleasures. Later they will be commanded to stop speaking against one another (4:11), complaining (5:9) and taking inappropriate oaths (v. 12). No evidence suggests that James was addressing non-Christians in this or any other passage of his epistle.

"Cleanse your hands, you sinners" (James 4:8) refers to a decisive act of repentance, a necessary step in the forgiveness process (2 Corinthians 7:9-10). Hands usually represent one's actions as opposed to the thoughts, represented by the heart, which James mentions next. "[P]urify your hearts, you double-minded" is the second half of a antithetic parallel poetic phrase, a common style in Hebrew poetry where the first clause is reflected or restated with slight alterations in the second. "Purify" and "cleanse" are equivalent concepts while "hands" and "heart" contrast one another; the first is external and the second internal. One accomplishes this command by obeying the truth (1 Peter 1:22).

James refers to his readers as sinners and "double-minded" (cf. James 1:8). Having made a commitment to Christ, they have since been seduced into loving the world and are now threatened with eternal condemnation unless they repent and return to Christ. James leaves no room for the idea that Christians cannot fall from grace. Instead, he pleads with them to recognize the severity of sin's consequences. This will produce genuine repentance, described in terms relating to ancient funeral practices: "Lament and mourn and weep!" (4:9a). Sorrow for sin is placed in stark contrast to the joy of living close to God (v. 8). "Let your laughter be turned to mourning and your joy to gloom" (v. 9b) confirms the serious nature of repentance.

Once again, the admonition is followed by an amazing promise: "Humble yourselves in the sight of the Lord, and He will lift you up" (James 4:10). The penitent individual seeking forgiveness before God is humbled before Him as he complies with God's clearly stated will. There, in His sight, the Lord will lift up the face bowed in submission. With this picture firmly in mind, the Christian is not likely soon to wander away from devotion to God, Who longs for a restored relationship with humanity. In fact, one would simply be foolish to reject true wisdom. Those who come to God will be given strength to stand in His presence, forgiven and prepared to do His will.

STUDY QUESTIONS

1. Describe the state of unrest in Chapter 4.

2. What caused these problems?

3. Why were their prayers ineffective?

4. What were their true motives in praying?

5. What is the price of friendship with the world?

6. Explain the main interpretations of James 4:5-6a.

7. Whom does James address as "sinners"? Why?

8. Whom does God resist?

9. How should God be approached?

10. What will be the end result of returning to God?

CHAPTER 11

Timely THOUGHTS

(JAMES 4:11-17)

Paramedics arrived at an apartment complex to find a middle-aged man suffering a heart attack. However, they couldn't enter the small apartment to stabilize the patient because of the man's Staffordshire bull terrier. He had trained the dog to attack because of the high crime rate. The dog did exactly what it was trained to do – protect its master – who died that day of a heart attack.[1] The precautions the man took to save his life cost him his life. Time, at least for him, ended. "Every moment comes to you pregnant with a divine purpose; time being so precious that God deals it out only second by second. Once it leaves your hands and your power to do with it as you please, it plunges into eternity, to remain forever what you made it."[2]

Time was being grossly mishandled by James' readers, who boasted of their faith but failed to live it. They were confident that they were safe simply because they were Christians. James gently reminds them of their need for complete obedience to God in every aspect of life. Urgency stirs among these commands and warnings because one never knows when time will run out.

JUDGING A BROTHER

With 4:11, James returns to the immediate context of his reader's lives: their past sins (vv. 1-2). Rather than continuing to fight, he admonishes them to exercise brotherly love. His words are strong,

"Do not speak evil of one another" (v. 11). Their conduct toward fellow Christians revealed a failure to practice the "royal law" (2:8). They are brethren, servants of the same God, before Whom they are to humble themselves that He may lift them up (4:10). Christians cannot remain humble before God while harshly judging a brother. When they engage in mutual character assassinations, they not only hurt the reputation of their brethren; they pass judgment against them. Do they really think they have that right? If one individual can determine the eternal fate of another, why do they need a divine standard of judgment? These readers act as if God can't perform this duty. They have judged the law of Christ as useless. This is "the word of truth" (James 1:18), "the implanted word, which is able to save your souls" (v. 21), and "the perfect law of liberty" (v. 25). Rather than serving under this law, the judging Christians have placed themselves over it, as a judge rather than a doer.

In an even more startling twist, James charges that the judgmental Christian is guilty of usurping a role that only God is qualified to occupy, that of Lawmaker. He alone holds the ultimate power "to save and to destroy" eternally (James 4:12). While Moses was the lawgiver of the Old Testament, James' reference here can be applicable only to Jesus Christ by Whose words all will ultimately be judged (Matthew 25:31ff; John 5:27). In light of all this, James pointedly asks, "Who are you to judge another?" In their judgmental spirit, these Christians have boldly dispatched as no longer useful their brethren, Scripture, God and Christ!

BOASTING ABOUT THE FUTURE

Turning to their future (James 4:13-15), James offers an imaginary example illustrating the danger of misplaced priorities. The phrase, "Come now" (v. 13), sometimes translated "go," was "a pointed call for attention that indicates the seriousness of what follows."[3] Having gained their attention, James tells of a traveling businessman who has contrived a highly structured strategy for his success. His confidence that success is on the horizon is obvious in his voice and demeanor.

A closer look at verse 13 reveals just how closely James' hypothetical businessman has prepared. He knew when he would start, today or tomorrow, "as if ye had the free choice of either day as a certainty." [4] He knew his new address, in "such and such a city," the duration of stay, "a year," the specific activity, "buy and sell" (the root word for the English "emporium") and even the outcome, "make a profit."

> So the picture is the picture of a man looking at a map. He points at a certain spot on it, and says, "Here is a new city where there are great trade chances. I'll go there; and I'll get in on the ground floor; and I'll trade for a year or so; and I'll make my fortune, and come back rich." [5]

He had done his homework and consequently displayed his self-congratulating pride for all to admire. Absolutely nothing was left to chance.

The imagery and description of the business operation accurately reflect the practices of James' day.

> We should be impressed that people in the first century world, far from being primitive, were quite the travelers. Roads, shipping and communications in the Roman Empire were well organized. ... Travel, while not comfortable or luxurious by modern standards, was nevertheless regularly done. The New Testament itself reveals the readiness with which Paul could travel great distances. [6]

His story had a ring of truth to it with which James' readers' could easily relate. Perhaps they knew someone very similar to the man James described or even saw a little of themselves in him.

The student should be cautioned against too harsh a judgment based on James' story. He is not seeking to condemn the rich. The attitude rebuked in this parable can afflict "[all] people, regardless of wealth, social standing or any other condition, who make their life plans without respect to the will of God." [7] He was not censuring those who make decisions that impact the future in an effort to conduct a successful business. Scripture approves legitimate profit (Acts 5:4; 2 Thessalonians 3:10), hard work (1 Thessalonians 4:11-12), providing for one's family (1 Timothy 5:8), attending to one's own business (Ephesians 4:28), and wise planning (Luke 14:28-32). The sin was in forgetting God while making plans for the future. James' businessman made room for the things of the world but not for God. His trust was in the physical as if he had no need for the spiritual – God – and in time as if he owned and controlled the future.

A well-known football coach, on vacation with his family in Maine, entered the local movie theater. As they took their seats for the afternoon show, everyone in the theater began to applaud. The coach, turning to his wife, said, "I can't believe people recognize me all the way up here." But then the man directly in front of them turned around to shake the coach's hand with this greeting: "Thanks for coming. They won't start the movie for less than 10 people." The coach, like James' businessman, had an over-inflated sense of his own importance. Unlike the coach, who was simply embarrassed, James' businessman found eternity was in the balance. His mistake was in not "considering the shortness and uncertainty of human life." [8]

No human can ever accurately see the future. Even the best-laid plans will fail to account for the unexpected element of chance or the fragile nature of life itself (Psalm 39:4-5; Ecclesiastes 9:11; Matthew 6:30; 1 Peter 1:24). "The only certain factor about human life is that it will end sooner or later in death." [9] The man in James' illustration could not know that he would see tomorrow, let alone a year down the road. Like the rich man in Luke 12:19, this man assumed that he would have many years ahead of him. To entrust one's soul on such an assumption is foolish.

Every man needs God because of tomorrow's uncertainty. When James asks, "For what is your life," he uses a phrase that in "some manuscripts reads, 'for what kind of life is yours.' " [10] James describes life as a vapor, mist or fog that appears but then suddenly vanishes. Without God it is hardly anything to boast over (Proverbs 27:1).

James contrasts the self-reliant attitude of the businessman with the humble, submissive mindset he endorses. Not knowing what the future holds, Christians rely upon the One who holds their future: "If the Lord wills," he writes, "we shall live and do this or that" (James 4:15; cf. Acts 18:21; 1 Corinthians 4:19; 16:7; Philippians 2:19, 24; Hebrews 6:3). Commentators debate whether James intended for his readers to verbalize their trust when speaking of the future. Most warn against using such a phrase in "an irreverent and flippant manner" [11] or

as "a charm." [12] James advocates that each believer plan and work together with God in complete dependence on Him. "No Christian can
safely assume that he can live independently of God. For a believer
to leave God out of his plans is an arrogant assumption of self-suffi-
ciency, a tacit declaration of independence from God." [13] The future belongs to those who truly belong to God. His is the only measure of success that will ultimately matter.

Paul Tournier is quoted as saying, "God gives me the gift of twenty-
four hours a day; yet he is kind enough to accept in return the little time
I give back to him." [14] For James' self-absorbed businessman, prideful
boasting in as yet unattained accomplishments devoured today so that
there was no room or apparent need left for God (James 4:16-17). He
made success on paper and boasted of those untried plans as if they had
already yielded his projected prosperity. There are occasions when one
should enjoy a measure of pride (1 Thessalonians 2:19; Galatians 6:14).
"All boasting is not evil, but 'all such glorying' … The type of glorying James had just outlined, in which men flaunted all kinds of ambi-
tions and godless plans without any reference whatever to Almighty
God, was reprehensible and sinful." [15] These boasts are defiant decla-
rations of independence from God. The example James cited illustrates
just this kind of man. As they tell it, one is led to conclude that these
successful, self-made businessmen "were the masters of their own
fate." [16] They alone were responsible for their successes.

All such boasting, James warns, is evil. The evil aspect of the boasting James condemns arises from the mistaken conclusion that one has
no need for God. It is an arrogance of human ability and blasphemy
against God. Not only does it lack "the quality of being good, it is
aggressively and viciously wicked." [17] God gives meaning to life and
no measure of human success will add anything to it in the end.

LIVING FOR CHRIST TODAY

There is always the danger of wasting today. Rather than filling it
with the boasts of what tomorrow supposedly holds, the Christian is
instructed to focus on living according to the values and commandments of Christ. These are always good in contrast to the evil of James
4:16. God expects nothing from Christians that is not, in the end, go-

ing to make them better. Christ also has not laid any hidden traps. He has clearly provided the church with a complete revelation of His will (Jude 3). Today, the Christian should seek to learn what is good so that it can be practiced. "Therefore, to him who knows to do good and does not do it, to him it is sin" (James 4:17). His statement indicates that the Christian has the skills to do good.

> If we know we should do this, yet fail to do it, we are clearly sinning. Of course, the principle is of broader application. In any area of life, the opportunity to do good makes us responsible to do it. If we know what is right, we are under obligation to live up to that light. Failure to do so is sin against God, against our neighbors, and against ourselves.[18]

James is saying, "'Now that I have pointed the matter out to you, you have no excuse.' Knowing what should be done obligates a person to do it."[19] This phrase in the original expresses an ongoing, continuous action. He is warning those who know the right way but persist in living the wrong way that they have no valid explanation for their sinful life. "These Christians knew that friendship with the world is enmity with God, that God resists the proud and gives grace to the humble, and so on. They knew better, they were not living up to the standard which they were capable (Luke 12:47; John 15:22)."[20] While the readers are urged to grow in their knowledge of God's Word, it is just as important for them to practice the truth that they learn.

Commentators have found wonderful insights in James' use of this illustration and in its placement in the letter itself. From the very beginning, James has placed great importance on obedience. He called for his readers to be "doers of the word" (James 1:22), to have a faith coupled with works of obedience (2:24), meanwhile working to curb the negative impact of the tongue (3:8), and to submit to God (4:7). James' message is inescapable; God's Word must be obeyed. Not to do so is to label it vain and to set oneself up as superior to His Word.

That need is just as pertinent today as it was when James first penned his letter. James' goal is not to create a burden of guilt on the shoulders of his readers because of their inadequacy to live a life of sinless perfection. Instead, he wants them to have a living, working faith that shapes their daily lives and enables them to look to a future, not of monetary success in a year down the road but of an eternal reward (James 1:12). The question for the Christian is, "How am I using today to obey and glorify God?" This is the message of James.

A few residents of Cape Coral, Fla., were shocked to learn that utility workers had inadvertently connected their water lines with wastewater from residential sinks and toilets. [21] In one case a family had been drinking this treated but substandard water for more than three months. Of course, residents were shocked and troubled by this revelation, and immediate steps were taken to correct the situation. Can anyone imagine those families telling the waterworks employees not to bother switching their water service back? Who would want to keep drinking polluted water just because they had grown accustomed to it? In the case of James' readers, they have just learned that what they were practicing was substandard Christianity: treating each other poorly (James 4:11), taking God for granted (v. 14), and failing to practice what they preached. For them to refuse to embrace this pure, inspired standard would be a grave mistake with eternal consequences.

There is no doubt that James' words brought considerable hope to his readers by reminding them of God's longing for their faithfulness (James 4:5), of His provision of all the resources they need to carry out His will (v. 8), of personally "lifting up" those who humble themselves before Him in submission (v. 10), and of empowering them to do the good they learn from Him (v. 17). For them to refuse what they have now learned would be a sin and a terrible waste of the short time remaining in their lives.

> It's up to me to use it.
> I must suffer if I lose it.
> Give account if I abuse it.
> Just a tiny little minute,
> But eternity is in it. [22]

STUDY QUESTIONS

1. How must James' audience conduct themselves toward one another?

2. How does one become guilty of judging the law?

3. What power does a lawgiver possess?

4. James refers to a hypothetical man in 4:13. What does he say about this man?

5. What mistake did this man make regarding his life?

6. What mistake did he make regarding God?

7. What makes his particular kind of boasting sinful?

8. In what did this man rejoice?

9. What responsibility comes with one's increased learning of the will of God?

10. Explain the concept of a sin of omission?

CHAPTER 12

THE HIGH *Cost* OF LOW LIVING

(JAMES 5:1-12)

It sounds like a scene from Laurel and Hardy or Abbott and Costello; an observant prisoner being transferred in St. Charles County, Mo., seized his opportunity to escape through a fire exit door in the jail parking lot. What the authorities knew but he didn't was that the door opened into a solid brick wall. He was treated for head injuries at a local hospital.[1] The wall created a notable barrier to his escape. As James' attention turns to the wealthy unbelievers who have historically, as a class, posed great barriers for the advancement of Christ's cause (James 2:6), he describes their imminent and inescapable condemnation (5:1-6).

Some identify the "rich" in James 5:1 as the Sadducees, the wealthy Jewish leaders of Jerusalem just prior to its destruction by the Romans in A.D. 70 and "notorious oppressors of the poor."[2] Clearly James has unbelievers, not wealthy Christians, in mind. He makes a clear distinction between the rich and his readers, the latter repeatedly being addressed as "brethren" (vv. 7, 9, 10, 12). James does not extend the gospel to the rich or call them to repent. The truth is that James is not actually addressing the wealthy but the poor Christians they are oppressing "that they may bear with patience the violence of the rich."[3] Verses 1-6 serve primarily as background for verses 7-12, but the inspired warning against "the love of money" (1 Timothy 6:10) is well worth the reader's consideration.

SINS OF THE WEALTHY

This section of James has been called a "searching and piercing ... denunciation of the sins of the rich," which has earned James such titles as "a prophet of social justice." [4] He boldly depicts their impending judgment (James 5:1-3a), using a familiar phrase to get his reader's attention ("come now"; cf. 4:13) and in describing their response to judgment ("weep and howl"; cf. 4:9). Yet he extends no hope to them, that prompts their response, a sudden outburst of grief. Their miserable state is described as wretched and their destruction certain (Hebrews 10:27). If they would listen to the Christian message and seriously consider the fate before them, "they would literally shriek over the prospect." [5]

What is to become of their beloved wealth? James declares that their riches, including money, precious metals, garments, oil, food, etc., would become corrupted. Moths ruin their vast closets of expensive clothes. "In both verbs ('corrupted' and 'moth-eaten) James uses a perfect tense .... . [The] deterioration had been going on and was still going on." [6] The precious gold and silver, cautiously stored and protected, are corroded. Their personal hopelessness is surrounded by waste. Certainly James has this in mind as he considers the great earthly wealth saved to no good end. Greed and covetousness poison the soul.

Three voices will testify against the greedy rich in James 5: rust, withheld wages and cheated widows. The first is the haunting cry for justice of their rusted wealth (v. 3) that will serve as evidence against them. The rust will also eat their flesh just as it ate away at their much-treasured wealth. The second voice cries out allegations of withheld wages. Those wages cry out from the hands of the greedy masters, and the cry was not in vain. The third voice reveals the dishonesty of the wealthy toward the rich, who cheat their workers of the rightful gain of their labors. The greed of their wealthy master's cry out for justice and no human seems willing or eager to rush to their defense.

Unheard by men on earth, God hears their cries in heaven. James leaps past the fact that God hears these cries to stress the greater point that it is the "Lord of Sabaoth" (hosts) who hears. This is one "of the most majestic of all the titles of God in the Old Testament" [7] (Isaiah 1:9; Psalm 46:7, 11). God is the Lord of Sabaoth because He commands all the hosts of heaven, an innumerable army of angels. The One who "commands the armies of heaven is strong on behalf of earth's downtrodden masses." [8] With these three witnesses, the ungodly will be consumed by a fire of their making.

CHARGES AGAINST THE WEALTHY

Four specific charges are leveled against these wealthy oppressors.

• **They have stored away the wrong kind of treasure** (James 5:3b; Matthew 6:19-21). While operating under the delusion that they were making provisions for their own future, they are in fact accumulating evidence that will be used in their own conviction before God. The "last days" refer to the period of time between Jesus' ascension and His second coming (Hebrews 1:1-2; Acts 2:17; 1 Peter 1:20).

• **They are guilty of cheating the poor** (James 5:4). Nathan the prophet touched the heart of King David with his story of a wealthy man, surrounded with abundance, stealing from a poor man (2 Samuel 12:1-15). Just as repugnant are the crimes committed by those in James 5. "These rich people thought of themselves as invincible, untouchable, able to steal from their employees and get away with it (James 5:4)." [9] James' familiarity with agricultural life is revealed twice in this passage. He mentions laborers rather than slaves and the mowing of fields, farming techniques peculiar to Palestine. [10] The poor farmhands worked in the fields of the rich and, according to the Jewish Law, they came to their employers at the end of the day to be paid (Leviticus 19:13; Deuteronomy 24:15). Their wages, however, were withheld by fraud.

The rich were robbing the poor (Malachi 3:5; Proverbs 19:17; 21:13). "When a poor man does any work in a house, the vapor proceeding from him, through the severity of his work, ascends towards heaven. Woe to his employer if he delay to pay him his wages." [11] With no human to protect them from the abuses of their oppressors, the poor have no other recourse than to turn to God.

• **Their lifestyle is selfish** (James 5:5). James paints a classic portrait of one who has loved the things of this world. Their goals and values were confined to the earthly (Colossians 3:2). Their lives are described in terms of pleasure and luxury. The word "pleasure" has been defined as "pampering the flesh" [12] and "disgustingly selfish." [13] The term "luxury" is defined as indulging one's "sinful and sensual appetites to the uttermost,"[14] "extravagantly wasteful, [and] going beyond pleasure to vice."[15] Using the imagery of a sacrificial animal gorging on its food oblivious to the fact that its life is about to end,[16] James says that the time of their judgment had come and God would have the final word regarding their fate.

• **They are charged with persecuting the church** (James 5:6). James' concern is deeper than just the "the rough, highhanded" mistreatment of the poor at the hands of their rich oppressors[17] (2:6-7). False charges would lead to their conviction and death.

Much ink has been spilt over the identity of the just of James 5:6. Two possibilities are offered: Jesus Christ (Acts 3:14; 7:52; 22:14) or Christians in general. If the "rich" are the Jewish leaders in Jerusalem, as many believe they are, who would dispute that "the great sin of the heartless rich being thus condemned and judged was that of murdering the Messiah?"[18] "The just" of 5:6, being singular, is thought to support this identification of Christ as the "*innocent man*, or righteous man."[19]

Others think the "just" refers to "all the innocent blood shed, and to be shed."[20] The word, then, translated "the just" (James 5:6), "is that class of people who were known as the righteous believers. And they came largely from the ranks of the poor."[21] Robertson argues that "the generic use of the singular with article for the class" indicates that James is thinking of a group of people rather than one individual.[22] This being true, the just simply did not have any recourse to resist the abuses of their superiors or have the courage to fight back (1 Peter 2:18-21; Matthew 5:38-45; Romans 12:19). "To protest might result in further brutality, or dismissal from their [much-needed] job."[23] But the abused "just" are not at the mercy of the merciless rich (James 5:7-12).

EXERCISE PATIENCE

In facing oppression, James counsels his readers, fellow Christians, to exercise patience (James 5:7-8). The word for "patience" means, "long suffering," enduring under the stress of hardship, "self-restraint that does not try to get even for a wrong that has been done."[24] This is possible for believers in situations when unbelievers may find it nearly impossible to bear because of their perspective of time and eternity. "[If] God, a holy God, can be patient with us in the face of the enormity of our sin, how much more can we be patient in the face of whatever opposition may come our way"? [25] With perspective, the believer will be ready for life and eternity.

Patience is illustrated in James' reference to the farmer, planting seeds and waiting through the early and latter rains. Anticipating and appreciating the harvest provides an incentive to endure the adversities represented by the rains. The harvest's " 'preciousness' (compare Psalm 126:6, 'precious seed') will more than compensate for all the past. Compare the same image, Galatians 6:3, 9." [26] The believer knows that enemies do not have the final word and that in God's time He will set the record straight. Just as the farmer can know that the Lord is going to send the rain for the crops, so we can know the Lord is going to send his Son once again; we can trust God for the final outcome of our lives.[27]

James calls for his readers, who are suffering wrong, to anticipate the second coming of the Lord. In contrast to the rich, who "have fattened [their] hearts as in a day of slaughter" (James 5:5b), the believers are commanded, "Establish your hearts," that is, "be strong in the inner man. … stand unmoved by trouble." [28] By focusing on the inner, spiritual person, the Christian will be ready for the coming of the Lord which James insists "is at hand" (v. 8). The fact that Jesus did not return during their lifetime is completely beside the point. Christians are urged to live each day in the realization that today could be the day of His longed-for coming (Matthew 25:13).

James warns of the danger of taking one's stress out on loved ones. When oppressed, be careful to treat fellow Christians with kindness. "Do not grumble," James cautions his readers, commanding them to stop their current practice of groaning against one another (James 5:9). Believers must be careful not to lower their conduct toward each other to the level of the unbelievers opposing them. "The believers are to be patient toward both outsiders who oppress them and insiders who irritate them." [29] To share the attitudes and actions of unbelievers can result only in sharing their condemnation as well. Judgment is near, both for the oppressor and oppressed. "[T]he Judge is standing at the door"; the believer is never alone.

James offers two examples of patience. The first is the Old Testament prophets (James 5:10). No single prophet is mentioned, but Jeremiah, the "weeping prophet," is a favorite among commentators. The fact is, every prophet "who spoke in the name of the Lord" suffered to some extent because of his devotion to God. Any one of them could serve as a model or pattern (Luke 6:47) for the believer.

His second example of the blessing that is attached to endurance comes from the familiar account of the suffering and patience of Job (James 5:11). Reading his ordeal in the Old Testament, one notes that Job's patience did not include silent resignation. It did include a refusal to abandon faith in God. Although everything he saw and heard seemed to indicate just the opposite, Job endured because of his firm belief that God in His time would act in Job's best interest (Job 42:10-17). Looking backward and evaluating Job's life, one can see his faith in God was completely justified. God was ultimately in control. The contrast in Job's case is striking. "The devil's end was to drive him to despair, and to cause him to blaspheme his Maker"; [30] God's end was to reward his faith (Job 42:10-15).

MAINTAIN HONESTY

The final admonition to the oppressed is to maintain honesty in speech (James 5:12). James' concern is over the believer's relationship with every oppressor. James here certainly quotes Jesus' teaching regarding swearing (Matthew 5:33-37). Neither he nor Jesus was forbidding oaths in legal settings. "Both Jesus (Matthew 8:12; 26:63) and Paul either used or submitted to oaths at various times (Romans 1:9; 1 Thess. 5:27)." [31]

Just what does James teach regarding oaths? Like Jesus, James lived in a world where the religious savvy could make all kinds of promises, sealed with an oath, and then break their word claiming a technicality of the oath not covered in the laws governing oaths (perhaps not unlike children making a promise with their crossed fingers hidden behind their backs). One might seek to escape oppression by taking a false or blasphemous oath. One may also be tempted to respond with an inappropriate use of God's name in anger toward enemies. Christians must not use suffering or difficulties as an excuse for sin.

A Wisconsin man, arrested in connection with the theft of a global positioning system, was captured because police were able to use the stolen GPS to track him down.[32] As Moses wrote long ago, "[B]e sure your sin will find you out" (Numbers 32:23). It is futile for one to think that he can escape accountability before God (Psalm 139:7-10). As Christians, we must strive to reflect the high moral standards of Christ rather than the low standards of the world. "The great Greeks held that the best guarantee of any statement was not an oath but the character of the man who made it; and that the ideal was to make ourselves such that no one would ever think of demanding an oath from us." [33] This is James' point; one's word should be so dependable that an oath should not be required to reinforce his or her promises.

Not just the character of the individual Christian is at stake. The world will judge the church, Christianity and Christ Himself by the words and actions of those who profess to follow Him. Believers must not be found guilty with the world or found by God to be hypocrites. The Lord will keep His promises. The Christian must keep his faith.

STUDY QUESTIONS

1. Who does James say will weep?

2. What does he say will happen to their riches?

3. What are the charges laid against them before God?

4. Identify the three voices speaking against the rich.

5. What does "Sabaoth" mean?

6. Define the terms "pleasure" and "luxury" (James 5:5).

7. Explain the phrase "fattened your hearts as in a day of slaughter."

8. To whom does the phrase "the just" refer?

9. What lessons do the prophets and Job teach?

10. What does James teach regarding oaths?

CHAPTER 13

A Sickness CALLED SIN

(JAMES 5:13-20)

One of the plays featured at Scotland's Edinburgh Fringe Festival was the hour long "Sweet FA," with no actors or script, just an empty stage.[1] Unlike that "play," Christianity involves real people with real problems being obedient to God in their everyday lives, as is evident in James' closing verses.

Scholars vastly differ as to the overall structure of James' epistle. Some think it is only a collection of unrelated proverbial sayings.[2] Others twist the text to prove their human doctrines (2 Peter 3:16). This is especially true with James 5:13-20, "one of the most disputed portions of the Epistle."[3] At least two common threads connect this passage with the overall message of the letter: prayer and sin. Prayer is mentioned seven times in James 5:13-20. When this thread is followed, the reader is impressed with the versatility and practical nature of prayer in the life of the faithful Christian: in trouble, joy or sickness, the Christian's first response should always be to pray (vv. 13-14; 1 Thessalonians 5:17).

Prayer is the appropriate response for the suffering Christian, although an oath may be the more natural response to oppression. "In James's view, oaths and prayers are simply the verbal expressions of underlying stances of unbelief and faith, respectively."[4] James uses the same word for "suffering" here that he used in regard to the Old Testament prophets (James 5:10). "The Jews taught that the meaning of the ordinance, Leviticus 13:45, which required the leper to cry, 'Unclean! unclean!' was, 'that thus making known his calamity, the people might be led to offer up prayers to God in his behalf.' " [5] When one is suffering, prayer is the prescribed antidote, and the Greek phrasing of James forms a command to continue in prayer.

The second scene, "Is anyone cheerful?" also depicts a response of praise to God: "Let him sing psalms" (James 5:13). At first this may not appear so profound, but in times of happiness one is subject to disregard a need for God. In those cases cheerfulness becomes dangerous. Even those with the most limited exposure to the faith can understand why Christians have just cause to rejoice. "He knows that his heavenly Father extends to him a standing invitation to draw near to Himself, which no experience of joy or sorrow and no conditions of prosperity or adversity have any power to cancel." [6] It is only natural for Christ's church to sing!

PRAY FOR THE SICK

James connects the need for prayer with illness in verse 14 as the afflicted Christian is given the responsibility of calling for the "elders of the church." This passage has been open to a wide range of interpretation and the unfortunate foundation for longstanding doctrines of the Roman Catholic Church. One popular view asserts that James promises that the elders' prayer and anointing will result in the physical healing of the sick. While it is obvious that this epistle, among the earliest documents of the New Testament, was written within the brief timeframe when miraculous gifts were still available, it is not at all certain that they were prevalent among James' original audience. Another view sees James calling for the elders to fulfill their ministry as shepherds of the church by praying for the sick in their congregation.

The word James uses for "sick" in James 5:14 literally means, "to be weak (without strength)," [7] and "helpless (Rom. 5:6)." [8] Upon the elders' arrival, they are to anoint the patient with oil. James selected the common word for rub or anoint rather than the "usual word for sacramental or ritualistic anointing." [9] Although oil was a common treatment (Isaiah 1:6; Mark 6:13; Luke 10:34), James does not indicate the specific type of oil or any other specific details. This supports the nearly unanimous conclusion of scholars that the oil is only incidental to the prayer.

James makes a powerful promise regarding the sick that is directly connected to the elders' prayer. In saying that the elders' prayer "will save the sick" (James 5:15) he means, " 'shall restore to physical health'; for the New Testament nowhere asserts that men are saved, in a spiritual sense, by prayer." [10] This must be the case unless James has some other kind of illness in mind, which he confirms that he does when he concludes, "And if he has committed sins, he will be forgiven" (v. 15b). Although the word translated "sick" in 5:14 "is usually used in reference to physical illness," in 5:15 the word is "only used for a spiritual condition" [11] (cf. Hebrews 12:3; Revelation 2:3). A careful examination of this text brings out the most difficult aspect posed to interpreters. "The healing of which James speaks is unconditional." [12] The ramifications are obvious: "if the sick called for the elders as directed here, and the elders did their duty, no one in the church would ever die!" [13]

James must be discussing the spiritually ill and penitent who call upon the elders. They are then anointed with the oil of God's Word (1 John 2:20, 27) in a symbolic sense, and prayer is offered in keeping with the teaching of this letter (and the entire New Testament).

> The promise of James 5:13-16 is absolute. The scripture says that when the elders of the church anoint the sin-sick soul with oil and prayed for him, he will be healed. There is no "perhaps" or "maybe" about it. He will be raised up. The anointing and the prayer never fail. If elders smear olive-oil on the forehead of a person who is physically sick and pray for him will the sick, in every case – unfailingly – get well? If not, then James must not be talking about diseases of the flesh. [14]

On many occasions one's physical illness had led to spiritual restoration, whether through introspection, realization of life's fragility, or confronting one's sinfulness (1 John 1:8-10).

This passage is translated within Catholicism to lend support to their Sacrament of Extreme Unction, first coined by Peter Lombard. [15] In their translation, "elders" become "priests" to add authority to their practice. The footnote then claims divine origin for a human doctrine: "See here a plain warrant of scripture for the Sacrament of Extreme Unction, that any controversy against its institution would be against the express words of the sacred text in the plainest terms." [16] There is no basis for their translation of this verse, and outside the circle of Catholicism it is unanimously rejected.

Amid the confusion posed by these alternate interpretations, the reader is left with the impression that James recognizes a connection between one's spiritual and medical needs. "Over the main portal of the great Presbyterian Medical Center in Manhattan, N.Y., there are engraved the words: "All healing is of God; physicians only bind up the wounds." [17] While modern Christians do not have the promise of miraculous gifts and healing at the hands of church leaders, they do have the wonderful reminder from James of the power of prayer. "[In] no circumstances of life is faith impossible; and therefore there is no situation in which Christians cannot resort to prayer." [18]

CONFESS AND PRAY

Prayer, according to James, must be allowed to take precedence over sin (James 5:16-18). The most accurate reading of 5:16 would include the word "therefore": "Confess [therefore] your trespasses to one another" indicates a connection between this verse and the previous passage regarding the elders praying for the sick.[19] It is possible that the sick individual has called the elders in order to confess his sins to them and ask for their prayers. Is James saying, "If the prayer of faith can have such a miraculous result … Christians should always pray for one another?" [20] Or is this confessing Christian the sick saint of verse 14?

James uses a different word for "sin" in James 5:16. [21] As James' epistle confirms, the original audience struggled with sin: prejudice, hypocrisy, boasting, evil speaking and a number of other serious sins that would require confession and prayer. "The two imperatives, Confess and pray, [both in the original call for] the habitual practice of openness in two activities. Caution should be observed though; confession should be made only to the extent that the sin is open." [22] Certainly, any trespasses that interfere with the church's ability to assemble and worship would fall within the confines of this verse (Matthew 5:23-24). However, James is not commanding his readers "to unbosom themselves completely even to chosen individuals in private." [23] One cannot afford to deny the existence of sin within the body of Christ. Sin must be recognized, repented of and confessed. The confessions are to be mutual. "Christians must use their discretion as to the extent to which, and the people to whom they are prepared to divulge their sins of thought, word and deed." [24]

The Christian's remedy for sin is repentance, confession and prayer (Acts 8:22). The prayer of which James speaks in James 5:16 is " 'supplication' … where the emphasis is on the sense of need." [25] There is no mention in Scripture of the Christian's need for a priest for confession (each Christian is a priest, and Jesus is the High Priest; 1 Peter 2:9; Hebrews 4:14). Catholic commentators use James 5:16 to justify their practice of Auricular Confession (the compulsory confession before a priest, A.D. 1215 [26]).

In the phrase, "that you may be healed," James uses a common word for healing, whether spiritual or physical.[27] His promise depends, however, on the "effective, fervent prayer of a righteous man." Looking back over the previous verses, James has demonstrated the versatility of prayer in the Christian's life. In this case too, he promises, prayer will work. "Effective," in Greek, is the root from which the English word "energy" is derived.[28] The Christian who fails to avail himself or herself of the blessings available in prayer makes the path in life even more difficult and dangerous.

Actor Sean Connery has amassed legions of fans in his long career, yet when a reporter asked him why he continued to act at the age of 62, Connery said, "Because I get the opportunity to be somebody better and more interesting than I am." [29] Christians are in the process of becoming like Jesus; no better pattern can ever be found, not even Elijah, whom James uses to illustrate prayer's power (James 5:17-18). Elijah is the epitome of a righteous man. Spared death, Elijah had gained legendary status in James' day among many of the Jewish people. "So wonderful did the achievements of Elijah seem to succeeding generations that he came to be regarded as semi-divine." [30]

James first dismantles the aura that Elijah was superhuman, insisting that he had "a nature like ours," [31] being "fallible and sinful." [32] James points out that the famous drought of 1 Kings 17–18 began and ended in answer to Elijah's prayer, information not supplied in the Old Testament account. The phrase, "he prayed earnestly," translates the words "prayed with prayer," showing the strong desire that filled Elijah's prayers. God answers prayers, then and now; for as long as time lasts God will be "in the business of answering prayers for folks just like us." [33]

DEMONSTRATE COMPASSION

Officials at the Shanghai Zoo had to send some tiger cubs born in captivity to a nature reserve in South Africa so that experts could teach them how to survive. The cubs could chase prey, but they did not know how to kill it.[34] Sometimes Christians, too, forget how to live like true Christians. James closes with a wonderful challenge to demonstrate compassion toward the fallen (James 5:19-20). He warns that even the most faithful Christian can fall away from the faith ("wanders from the truth") and be eternally lost (1 Corinthians 10:12-13). Those who come to James holding the human doctrine of the security of the saints must redefine words, such as "brethren," to continue holding their beliefs. James indicates not only that Christians can fall away from the faith, but also that it happens fairly regularly. With so much at stake, James calls for mutual vigilance.

The believer's life is to be guided by God's Word (James 1:18-22). When that focus is lost, one will wander away from the truth. That soul will need someone to help turn him back to the life he should be living as a faithful Christian.[35] Who will love that one enough to become involved? James says that it only takes one spiritual, caring individual (5:19; cf. Galatians 6:1). When successful, that courageous Christian needs to be reassured just "how immense is the significance and how far-reaching are the consequences of the work he has accomplished." [36] That one has helped save an invaluable soul from eternal condemnation.

Clarke wrote, "Every man who knows the worth of his own should labor for the salvation of others. To be the means of depriving hell of her expectation, and adding even one soul to the Church triumphant, is a matter of infinite moment." [37] What a wonderful thought to leave in the minds of James' readers. The restoration of an unfaithful believer will involve God's covering "a multitude of sins" (James 5:20b). The sins covered, removed from sight, are those of the one restored.

A few commentators contend that James is teaching that in converting another, the soul-winner's sins are covered. But what if the backsliding Christian refuses to repent? Could one restore a sufficient number of backsliders to require Christ's atoning blood no longer for his or her own salvation? "It is very strange that Christian commentators should ever have thought that … James is advocating the recall of the backslider on the ground of the benefits it confers upon him." [38]

The epistle of James closes with one of Jesus' most powerful teachings: "For what profit is it to a man if he gains the whole world, and loses his own soul? Or what will a man give in exchange for his soul?" (Matthew 16:26). He calls each Christian to seek those who fall away that they may renew their lost hope with the promise that God will cover their sins. Then the letter abruptly ends. "For all its apparent abruptness this ending is wonderfully arresting; it sounds a call in the ears of Christian men and women which they ought most carefully to heed, and to which they should be most eager to respond." [39] It is the gospel of Christ reverberating through one who loved Him first as a brother, then as Lord and Savior. Jesus' mission became the life's work of James and the hope of all humanity. "[F]or the Son of Man has come to seek and to save that which was lost" (Luke 19:10).

STUDY QUESTIONS

1. Describe the comparisons of James 5:13.

2. What are the elders to do for the sick?

3. What is promised to "save the sick"?

4. What is the nature of the sickness in James 5:14?

5. What are the benefits of confessions?

6. How have these verses been abused?

7. How does James describe Elijah?

8. What lesson is taught by Elijah's example?

9. Does James teach that the Christian can be lost? Explain.

10. Whose sin is forgiven in 5:20? Why?

ENDNOTES

FOREWORD

1. James B. Adamson, *James, The Man & His Message* (Grand Rapids, MI: William B. Eerdmans, 1989) ix.

CHAPTER 1

1. R.V.G. Tasker, *The General Epistle of James* (Grand Rapids, MI: William B. Eerdmans, 1976) 13.

2. Adam Clarke, *Clarke's Commentary on the Old Testament*, Quickverse 7.0 CD-ROM (Cedar Rapids, IA: Parsons Technology, 2000).

3. Earl D. Radmacher, ed., *The Nelson Study Bible*, New King James Version (Nashville, TN: Thomas Nelson, 1997) 2102.

4. Harold L. Willmington, exec. ed., *The Open Bible* (Nashville, TN: Thomas Nelson, 1998) 1997.

5. *Nelson's Complete Book of Bible Maps & Charts* (Nashville, TN: Thomas Nelson, 1982) 454.

6. Adamson viii.

7. "PETA," *Firm Foundation* April 2003: 32.

8. Adamson viii.

9. Adamson vii.

10. William Barclay, *The Letters of James and Peter* (Philadelphia, PA: Westminster P, 1976) 8.

11. D. Edmond Hiebert, *An Introduction to the Non-Pauline Epistles* (Chicago: Moody P, 1962) 38.

12. Barclay 9.

13. Adamson 9.

14. Clarke.

15. William Byron Forbush, ed., *Fox's Book of Martyrs* (Philadelphia, PA: John C. Winston Co., 1926) 3.

16. Tasker 21.

17. Adamson 10.

18. Craig S. Keener, *The IVP Bible Background Commentary*, New Testament (Downers Grove, IL: InterVarsity P, 1993) 686.

19. Adamson 7.

20. "The Brother of God," Ukrainian Orthodoxy 12 Feb. 2007 <http://www.unicorne.org/orthodoxy/articles/calendar/novembre_5.htm>.

21. Richard Shenkman and Kurt Reiger, *One Night Stands With American History: Odd, Amusing, and Little-Known Incidents* (New York: Perennial, 2003) 179.

22. J.W. Roberts, *A Commentary on the General Epistle of James* (Austin, TX: R.B. Sweet Co., 1963) 10.

23. Adamson 14.

24. Tasker 27.

25. Roberts 24.

26. Flavius Josephus, *The Works of Josephus*, Antiquities 20. 9.1 199-203, Whiston, William, trans., Logos Research Systems, Inc. CD-ROM (Oak Harbor, WA: Hendrickson Publishers, 1997).

27. James Orr, ed., *International Standard Bible Encyclopedia*, Quickverse 7.0 CD-ROM (Cedar Rapids, IA: Parsons Technology, 2000).

28. Orr.

29. Orr.

30. Chuck Shepherd, "Leading Economic Indicators" *News of the Weird* (25 July 2004) 13 Feb. 2007 <http://www.newsoftheweird.com/archive/nw040725.html>.

31. Orr.

32. Everett Ferguson, ed., *Encyclopedia of Early Christianity* (New York: Garland, 1990) 483.

CHAPTER 2

1. Bob Fenster, *Duh! The Stupid History of the Human Race* 2004 Calendar (Kansas City, MO: Andrews McMeel, 2003) 29 Sept. 2003.

2. "Potpourri," *Firm Foundation* April 2003: 26.

3. Donald Guthrie, ed., *The New Bible Commentary* Revised (Grand Rapids, MI: Wm. B. Eerdmans, 1973) 1222.

4. James Burton Coffman, "Commentary on James," *Coffman Commentaries on the Old and New Testament,* Abilene Christian UP, 3 Jan. 2007 <http://www.searchgodsword.org/com/bcc/>.

5. Adamson 18.

6. Tasker 31.

7. Guthrie 1222.

8. Coffman.

9. Roberts 19-20.

10. William MacDonald, ed., *Believer's Bible Commentary: Old and New Testaments,* Logos Library System CD-ROM (Nashville, TN: Thomas Nelson, 1997).

11. Barclay 35.

12. *IVP New Testament Commentaries*, Online Commentary (Chicago: InterVarsity P, 2007) 12 Feb. 2007 <http://www.bible gateway.com/resources/commentaries/index.php?action=getBookSections& cid=13&source=>.

13. Frank E. Gaebelein, gen. ed., *The Expositor's Bible Commentary*, Zondervan Reference Software (Grand Rapids, MI: Zondervan, 1998).

14. Clarke.

15. Gaebelein.

16. "What, Us Worry?" *Firm Foundation* April 2003: 28.

17. Barclay 43.

18. Guy N. Woods, *A Commentary on the Epistle of James* (Nashville, TN: Gospel Advocate, 1978) 36.

19. "KneEmail," Mike Benson, ed. (Evansville, IN: Oak Hill Church of Christ, 2002) 352.

20. Archibald Thomas Robertson, *Word Pictures in the New Testament* (Nashville, TN: Broadman Press, 1933) 12.

21. Clarke.

22. Barclay 44.

23. Woods 40.

24. Roberts 46.

25. Robertson 13.

26. Clarke.

27. Coffman.

28. Clarke.

29. Marvin R. Vincent, *Word Studies in the New Testament* vol. 1 (Peabody, MA: Hendrickson Publishers, n.d.) 725.

30. Tasker 41.

31. "Around the Port in 130 Days," Cable News Network (21 Feb. 2003) 12 Feb. 2007 <http://www.cnn.com/2003/WORLD/sailing/02/21/yachtsman/index.html>.

32. Coffman.

33. Robert Jamieson, "Commentary on James," *Commentary Critical and Explanatory on the Whole Bible*, Abilene Christian UP, 3 Jan. 2007 <http://www.searchgodsword.org/com/jfb/>.

34. Gaebelein.

35. Roberts 57.

36. MacDonald.

CHAPTER 3

1. Robertson 17.

2. Gaebelein.

3. Coffman.

4. Cecil May Jr., ed., "Adding to the Worship," *Preacher Talk,* Magnolia Bible College, Aug. 1990: 2. The five elements of worship May mentions include singing, prayer, giving, communion and exhortation or preaching.

5. Harold S. Kushner, *When Bad Things Happen to Good People* (New York: Avon, 1983) 87.

6. Rick Sidorowicz, "Words and Wisdom, Seven Greatest Quotations" (Refresher, 1999) 12 Feb. 2007 <http://www.refresher.com/greatest 7.html>.

7. MacDonald.

8. Jamieson.

9. Jamieson.

10. Tomer Shiran, "Ornamental Hermit" (9 Apr. 2003) 12 Feb. 2007 <http://www.hermitary.com/around/archives/000037.html>.

11. MacDonald.

12. MacDonald.

13. Jamieson.

14. Clarke.

15. MacDonald.

16. Jamieson.

17. Vincent 729.

18. Jamieson.

19. Tasker 46.

20. MacDonald.

21. Woods 62.

22. Jerry Falwell, ed., Edward E. Hinson and Michael Kroll Woodrow, gen. eds., *KJV Bible Commentary,* Logos Library System CD-ROM (Nashville, TN: Thomas Nelson, 1997).

23. Jamieson.

24. MacDonald.

25. "KneEmail" 391.

26. Gaebelein.

27. Coffman.

CHAPTER 4

1. *IVP*.

2. MacDonald.

3. Woods 75.

4. Mark Dunagan, *James,* 24 Jan. 2007 <http://www.ch-of-christ.beaverton.or.us/James.html>.

5. "The Unsinkable Titanic," *Reader's Digest* April 1986: 125-128.

6. Tasker 50.

7. Roberts 70.

8. MacDonald.

9. Jamieson.

10. Woods 75.

11. Woods 74.

12. Spiros Zodhiates, *The Hebrew-Greek Key Study Bible*, New American Standard Version (Chattagooga, TN: AMG, 1990) 1861.

13. Clarke.

14. Woods 77.

15. Dunagan.

16. Barclay 57.

17. Barclay 57.

18. Radmacher 2106.

19. Barclay 57.

20. Tasker 52.

21. "Hate," *Firm Foundation* April 2003: 29.

22. Keener 693.

23. MacDonald.

24. MacDonald.

25. Gaebelein.

26. Frank Chesser, *The Spirit of Liberalism* (Huntsville, AL: Publishing Designs, 2001) 49.

27. "Policeman Tackles Actor in Role of Thief," *RedOrbit News* (8 Aug. 2004) 12 Feb. 2007 <http://www.redorbit.com/modules/news/tools.php?tool=print&id=77565>.

28. Tasker 54.

29. MacDonald.

30. Tasker 54.

31. Guthrie 1227.

32. Vincent 736.

33. Vincent 735.

34. Keener 693.

35. Clarke.

36. Tasker 54.

37. Jamieson.

38. Clarke.

CHAPTER 5

1. *The New Analytical Bible*, King James Version (Chicago: John A. Dickson, 1973) 16.

2. Gaebelein.

3. Geoffrey Herbert Crump, "Religious Routine," *Firm Foundation* May 2003: 28.

4. Gaebelein.

5. Woods 105.

6. Gaebelein.

7. Robertson.

8. MacDonald.

9. Gaebelein.

10. Vincent 738.

11. Barclay 64.

12. Woods 108.

13. Tasker 57.

14. Forbush 19.

15. Robertson.

16. Coffman.

17. Clarke.

18. MacDonald.

19. "KneEmail" 418.

20. Spiros Zodhiates, ed., *AMG Complete Word Study Reference CD*, CD-ROM (Chattanooga, TN: AMG Publishers, 1997), "implying necessity in accordance with the nature of things or with the divine appointment and therefore certain."

21. Falwell.

22. Guthrie 1228.

23. Vincent 743, quoting Chrysostum.

24. Alfred de Montesquiou, "Britons Fear Spiders More Than Terrorists, Survey Finds," *The Santa Fe New Mexican* (12 Oct. 2004) 12 Feb. 2007 <http://www.freenewmexican.com/news/5330.html>.

CHAPTER 6

1. Jon Callas, "Hatfields and McCoys Sign Truce," *The Mail Archive* (14 June 2003) 12 Feb. 2007 <http://www.mail-archive.com/eristocracy@merrymeet.com/msg00207.html>.

2. Strat Douthat, "Peace in the Valley," *The Commercial Appeal* [Memphis] 1 Aug. 1982.

3. "McCoy's Beat Hatfield Guns," *Anderson Bulletin* [Anderson, IN] 15 Feb. 1984.

4. Clarke.

5. Adamson xi.

6. Steve Mason, *Josephus and the New Testament* (Peabody, MA: Hendrickson, 1992) 177.

7. Roberts 9-10.

8. Tasker 23.

9. Ferguson 419.

10. Tasker 28.

11. Barclay 12.

12. Mason 178.

13. Roberts 10.

14. Tasker 23.

15. Forbush 3.

16. Roberts 9.

17. Barclay 5.

18. Leon Morris, *The Epistle to the Romans* (Grand Rapids, MI: William B. Eerdmans, 1988) 58.

19. Lewis W. Spitz, *The Protestant Reformation: 1517-1559* (New York: Harper and Row, 1985) 64.

20. Tasker 14.

21. Adamson ix-x.

22. F.F. Bruce, *The Epistle of Paul to the Romans*, R.V.G. Tasker, ed. (Grand Rapids, MI: Wm. B. Eerdmans, 1963) 109.

23. Woods 148.

24. Woods 148.

25. Lawrence O. Richards, *The Teacher's Commentary* (Colorado Springs, CO: Chariot Victor, 1987) 1016.

26. Moses Lard, *Commentary on Paul's Letter to the Romans* (Delight, AR: Gospel Light, nd) 123-124.

27. Coffman.

28. Woods 130.

29. Martin Luther, *A Treatise on Good Works*, Project Wittenberg and ICLnet (28 Dec. 1996) 12 Feb. 2007 <http://www.iclnet.org/pub/resources/text/wittenberg/wittenberg-luthworks.html>.

30. Martin Luther, *An Introduction to St. Paul's Letter to the Romans*, 3 Jan. 2007 <http://www.iclnet.org/pub/resources/text/wittenberg/wittenberg-luther.html#comment>.

31. Roberts 118.

32. Roberts 118.

33. Woods 131.

34. Lard 124.

35. Barclay 74.

CHAPTER 7

1. Arthur Sower, "Missing Record," *House to House, Heart to Heart*, Ronald Bartanen, ed. [Arthur Church of Christ, Arthur, IL] 22 June 2003.

2. Martin Luther, "Preface to the Letter of St. Paul to the Romans" *A Puritan's Mind* 12 Feb. 2007 <http://www.apuritansmind.com/Reformation/MartinLutherPrefaceRomans.htm>.

3. "Real Living According to James," unpublished and uncredited Bible class material 4.

4. Woods 133.

5. Clarke.

6. Gaebelein.

7. Woods 134-135.

8. Coffman.

9. Woods 137.

10. Woods 140.

11. Woods 140.

12. Roberts 110.

13. Tasker 67.

14. Guthrie 1229.

15. Coffman.

16. Geoffrey W. Bromiley, *The International Standard Bible Encyclopedia* vol. 4 (Grand Rapids, MI: William B. Eerdmans, 1988) 53.

17. Woods 150.

18. Robertson 38.

19. Vincent 745.

20. Adamson 134.

21. Johnny Hester, "Doing Good," *The Shady Acres Servant* [Shady Acres Church of Christ, Sikeston, MO] 15 Aug. 2004.

CHAPTER 8

1. Jeff Hecht, "Tongue Piercing Causes Brain Abscess," *New Scientist* (13 Dec. 2001) 12 Feb. 2007 <http://www.newscientist.com/article.ns?id=dn1689>.

2. Woods 154.

3. Roberts 129.

4. MacDonald.

5. Robertson.

6. Dunagan.

7. Robertson.

8. Gaebelein.

9. MacDonald.

10. Clarke.

11. *IVP*.

12. Barclay 88.

13. Clarke

14. *IVP*.

15. Coffman.

16. Roberts 131.

17. Gaebelein.

18. Coffman.

19. Clarke.

20. "Chief Traffic Cop Fired for Speeding," *Arutz Sheva, Israel National News* (11 Oct. 2004) 12 Feb. 2007 <http://www.israelnational news.com/print.php3?what=news&id=70222>.

21. Clarke.

22. Woods 178.

23. Adamson 23.

24. Woods 177.

25. Coffman.

26. Chuck Shepherd, "Updates" *Chuck Shepherd's News of the Weird* (6 July 2003) 12 Feb. 2007 <http://www.newsoftheweird.com/archive/ nw030706.html>.

CHAPTER 9

1. "Thomas Edison," Wikipedia, the Free Encyclopedia, 12 Feb. 2007 <http://en.wikipedia.org/wiki/Thomas_Edison>.

2. Vincent 753.

3. Gaebelein.

4. Robertson.

5. Robertson.

6. Woods 181.

7. Willmington.

8. Gaebelein.

9. R.C. Sproul, gen. ed., *New Geneva Study Bible*, Logos Library System CD-ROM (Nashville, TN: Thomas Nelson, 1997) c1995.

10. William F. Arndt and F. Wilbur Gingrich, *A Greek-English Lexicon of the New Testament and Other Early Christian Literature* (Chicago: University of Chicago P, 1952) 309.

11. MacDonald.

12. Gaebelein.

13. Robertson.

14. *IVP*.

15. Dunagan.

16. Robertson.

17. *IVP*.

18. *IVP*.

19. MacDonald.

20. Henry.

21. Jamieson.

22. Dunagan.

23. Jeff Chiu, "Artist finally agrees to repair her 'unimportant' gaffes" *USA Today* (15 Oct. 2004) 12 Feb. 2007 <http://www.usatoday.com/news/offbeat/2004-10-15-misspelling_x.htm>.

24. Coffman.

25. Gaebelein.

26. Henry.

27. Gaebelein.

28. MacDonald.

29. Sproul.

30. Jamieson.

31. Clarke.

32. Jamieson.

33. Robertson.

34. Sproul.

35. Gaebelein.

36. Sproul.

37. Roberts 148.

38. Dunagan.

39. Robertson.

40. Barclay 114.

41. Dunagan.

42. "Tank" Tankersly, "A Good Idea," *Park Avenue News* [Park Avenue Church of Christ, Memphis, TN] 5 Feb. 1989. Einstein's thought continues: "One, I'm sure, was the theory of relativity. I forget just what the other one was, but I think it had something to do with the demerits of broccoli."

43. Sproul.

CHAPTER 10

1. "PETA Shows Its Stripes With Letter to Arafat" *Los Angeles Daily News* via *Tom Gross Mideast Media Analysis* (20 Feb. 2003) 12 Feb. 2007 <http://www.tomgrossmedia.com/mideastdispatches/archives/000239.html>.

2. Guthrie 1231.

3. Dunagan.

4. Clarke.

5. Robertson 49.

6. MacDonald.

7. Mike Williams, "Greed – A Four-Letter Word (and the Virtues of Contentment)," *The Motley Fool* (22 Sept. 1997) 12 Feb. 2007 <http://www.fool.com/Fribble/1997/Fribble970922.htm>.

8. Coffman.

9. Barclay 115.

10. Gaebelein; cf. Clarke.

11. Coffman.

12. Roberts 159.

13. MacDonald.

14. Jamieson.

15. Radmacher 2109.

16. Dunagan.

17. Gaebelein.

18. Gaebelein.

19. Barclay 106.

CHAPTER 11

1. "Guard Dog Chases Medics," *Dog Hobbyist* (Reuters 30 July 2003) 13 Feb. 2007 <http://forums.doghobbyist.com/view.php?id=14922, 14922>.

2. Edythe Draper, *Draper's Book of Quotations*, WORDsearch Bible Study Software CD-ROM (Austin, TX: iExalt, 2000).

3. Gaebelein.

4. Jamieson.

5. Barclay 133.

6. Dunagan.

7. Coffman.

8. Clarke.

9. Tasker 102.

10. Jamieson.

11. Coffman.

12. Robertson.

13. Gaebelein.

14. Draper.

15. Coffman.

16. MacDonald.

17. Gaebelein.

18. MacDonald.

19. Gaebelein.

20. Dunagan.

21. "Fla. Homes Mistakenly Given Wastewater" *RedOrbit News* (31 July 2003) 13 Feb. 2007 <http://www.redorbit.com/news/display/?id=10156>.

22. Draper.

CHAPTER 12

1. Chuck Shepherd, "Least Competent Criminals" *Chuck Shepherd's News of the Weird* (7 Sept. 2003) 13 Feb. 2007 <http://www.news oftheweird.com/archive/nw030907.html>.

2. Coffman.

3. Jamieson.

4. MacDonald.

5. Roberts 182.

6. Roberts 183.

7. Tasker 113.

8. MacDonald.

9. Dunagan.

10. Roberts 186.

11. Clarke.

12. Clarke.

13. *IVP.*

14. Clarke.

15. *IVP*.

16. MacDonald.

17. MacDonald.

18. Coffman.

19. *IVP*.

20. Jamieson.

21. Gaebelein.

22. Robertson.

23. MacDonald.

24. Gaebelein.

25. Dunagan.

26. Jamieson.

27. Dunagan.

28. Gaebelein.

29. Gaebelein.

30. Clarke.

31. Dunagan.

32. "Man charged with stealing tracking device," *USA Today* (2 Sept. 2003) 13 Feb. 2007 <http://www.usatoday.com/tech/news/2003-09-02-stolen-gps_x.htm>.

33. Barclay 127.

CHAPTER 13

1. "You Couldn't Make It Up," *Edinburgh Festivals* (16 July 2003) 13 Feb. 2007 <http://www.edinburgh-festivals.com/topics.cfm?tid= 924&id=740172003>.

2. James L. Mays, ed., *Harper's Bible Commentary* (San Francisco: Harper and Row, 1988) 1272.

3. MacDonald.

4. *IVP*.

5. Clarke.

6. Tasker 126.

7. Robertson.

8. Guthrie 1235.

9. Gaebelein.

10. Tasker 132.

11. Dunagan.

12. H.A. (Buster) Dobbs, "Is Any Among You Sick?", *Firm Foundation* June 2004: 5.

13. Roberts 303.

14. Dobbs 5.

15. Guthrie 1235.

16. Tasker 128.

17. Coffman.

18. Tasker 132.

19. Jamieson.

20. Tasker 134.

21. Tasker 134; "slips, or lapses, rather than of willful sins," although he concedes that the words are used interchangeably.

22. Falwell.

23. Tasker 135.

24. Tasker 135.

25. Roberts 306.

26. Dunagan.

27. Dunagan.

28. Falwell.

29. "KneEmail" 478.

30. Tasker 140.

31. Clarke.

32. Coffman.

33. Dunagan.

34. "Shanghai Tiger Cubs Head for Survival Training," *China Daily* (29 Oct. 2004) 13 Feb. 2007 <http://www.china.org.cn/english/2004/Oct/110709.htm>.

35. Dunagan.

36. Tasker 143.

37. Clarke.

38. Tasker 143.

39. Tasker 144.